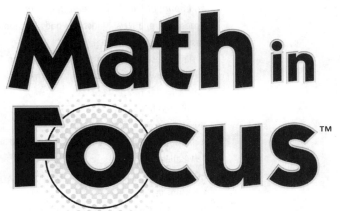

Math in Focus™

Singapore Math
by Marshall Cavendish

Extra Practice
5B

Author
Bernice Lau Pui Wah

Marshall Cavendish
Education

GReaT SOURCE®
HOUGHTON MIFFLIN HARCOURT
Supplemental Publishers

© 2009 Marshall Cavendish International (Singapore) Private Limited

Published by Marshall Cavendish Education
An imprint of Marshall Cavendish International (Singapore) Private Limited
Times Centre, 1 New Industrial Road, Singapore 536196
Customer Service Hotline: (65) 6411 0820
E-mail: tmesales@sg.marshallcavendish.com
Website: www.marshallcavendish.com/education

Distributed by
Great Source
A division of Houghton Mifflin Harcourt Publishing Company
181 Ballardvale Street
P.O. Box 7050
Wilmington, MA 01887-7050
Tel: 1-800-289-4490
Website: www.greatsource.com

First published 2009
Reprinted 2010, 2011

Math in Focus Extra Practice 5B
ISBN 978-0-669-01587-4

Printed in United States of America

3 4 5 6 7 8   1897   16 15 14 13 12 11
4500279300   B C D E

Contents

Decimals

Multiplying and Dividing Decimals

Introducing

Math in Focus™

Extra Practice

Extra Practice 5A and *5B*, written to complement *Math in Focus™: Singapore Math by Marshall Cavendish* Grade 5, offer further practice very similar to the Practice exercises in the Student Books and Workbooks for on-level students.

Extra Practice provides ample questions to reinforce all the concepts taught, and includes challenging questions in the Put on Your Thinking Cap! pages. These pages provide extra non-routine problem-solving opportunities, strengthening critical thinking skills.

Extra Practice is an excellent option for homework, or may be used in class or after school. It is intended for students who simply need more practice to become confident, or secure students who are aiming for excellence.

Name: _____   Date: _____

CHAPTER 8 Decimals

Lesson 8.1   Understanding Thousandths

Write the decimal shown in each place-value chart.

1.

Ones	Tenths	Hundredths	Thousandths
○ ○		○ ○ ○ ○	○ ○ ○ ○ ○

_____

2.

Ones	Tenths	Hundredths	Thousandths
○ ○ ○ ○ ○ ○	○ ○ ○		○ ○ ○ ○ ○ ○ ○ ○

_____

3.

Ones	Tenths	Hundredths	Thousandths
	○	○ ○ ○ ○ ○ ○ ○	○ ○ ○ ○ ○

_____

Mark an X to show where each decimal is located.

4. 0.063   **5.**   0.075   **6.**   0.082   **7.**   0.098

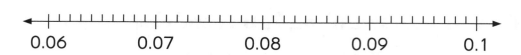

0.06   0.07   0.08   0.09   0.1

Write the decimal shown by each arrow.

8.

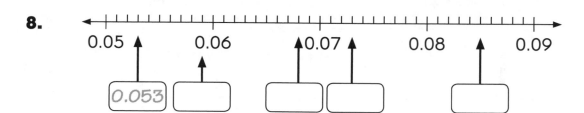

0.05   0.06   0.07   0.08   0.09

0.053

9.

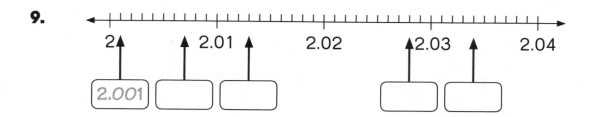

2   2.01   2.02   2.03   2.04

2.001

Complete.

10.   6 hundredths = _____ thousandths

11.   2 tenths 12 thousandths = _____ thousandths

12.   580 thousandths = _____ hundredths

13.   703 thousandths = 7 tenths _____ thousandths

14.   0.727 = 7 tenths _____ hundredths 7 thousandths

15.   0.094 = _____ tenths 9 hundredths _____ thousandths

● **Write the equivalent decimal.**

16. 9 thousandths = _____ **17.** 25 thousandths = _____

18. 416 thousandths = _____ **19.** 1,055 thousandths = _____

Write each fraction or improper fraction as a decimal.

20. $\frac{5}{1000}$ = _____ **21.** $\frac{78}{1000}$ = _____

22. $\frac{110}{1000}$ = _____ **23.** $\frac{603}{1000}$ = _____

24. $\frac{2508}{1000}$ = _____ **25.** $\frac{2640}{1000}$ = _____

26. $\frac{3009}{1000}$ = _____ **27.** $\frac{4567}{1000}$ = _____

● **Write each mixed number as a decimal.**

28. $1\frac{4}{1000}$ = _____ **29.** $3\frac{82}{1000}$ = _____

30. $5\frac{606}{1000}$ = _____ **31.** $7\frac{190}{1000}$ = _____

Complete.

32. 0.217 = _____ thousandths

33. 0.006 = _____ thousandths

34. 0.095 = _____ thousandths

35. 1.702 = _____ thousandths

**2.345 can be written in expanded form as $2 + \dfrac{3}{10} + \dfrac{4}{100} + \dfrac{5}{1000}$.
Write each decimal in expanded notation.**

36. $8.764 = $ ⬜ $+$ ⬜ $+$ ⬜ $+$ ⬜

37. $3.523 = $ ⬜ $+$ ⬜ $+$ ⬜ $+$ ⬜

**8.765 can be written in expanded form as $8 + 0.7 + 0.06 + 0.005$.
Write each decimal in expanded notation.**

38. $5.213 = $ _____ $+$ _____ $+$ _____ $+$ _____

39. $1.945 = $ _____ $+$ _____ $+$ _____ $+$ _____

Complete.

In 9.407,

40. the digit 7 is in the _____ place.

41. the value of the digit 0 is _____.

42. the digit 4 is in the _____ place.

43. the digit 9 stands for _____.

Lesson 8.2   Comparing and Rounding Decimals

Compare the decimals in each place-value chart.

Fill in the blanks. Write > or < in the .

1.

Ones	Tenths	Hundredths	Thousandths
5	0	7	8
4	0	8	7

_____ is greater than _____.

_____ ◯ _____

2.

Ones	Tenths	Hundredths	Thousandths
0	6	5	4
0	9	4	5

_____ is less than _____.

_____ ◯ _____

3.

Ones	Tenths	Hundredths	Thousandths
4	2	7	0
4	7	2	0

_____ is greater than _____.

_____ ◯ _____

Write >, <, or = in each ◯.

4.   0.589 ◯ 0.859   **5.**   3.409 ◯ 3.094

6.   0.065 ◯ 0.605   **7.**   9.10 ◯ 9.06

Circle the greatest decimal and underline the least.

8.   5.609   5.69   5.069   5.6

9.   80.002   80.02   80.2   80.202

Order the decimals from least to greatest.

10.   0.965, 0.956, 0.569   _____

11.   6.309, 9.036, 6.903   _____

12.   0.8, 0.088, 0.808, 0.88   _____

13.   0.029, 0.1, 0.999, 1   _____

Name: _____   **Date:** _____

Write the missing decimal in each box. Round the given decimal to the nearest hundredth.

14.

4.32

4.323

4.323 rounded to the nearest hundredth is _____.

15.

7.01

7.008

7.008 rounded to the nearest hundredth is _____.

Fill in the blanks.

16.   The length of a piece of rope is 3.458 meters.
Round the length to the nearest hundredth of a meter.

3.458 meters rounds to _____ meters.

17.   The mass of a dog is 12.015 kilograms.
Round the mass to two decimal places.

_____ kilograms rounds to _____ kilograms.

18.   The volume of milk in a carton is 2.295 liters.
Round the volume to the nearest hundredth of a liter.

_____ liters rounds to _____ liters.

Round each decimal to the nearest whole number, nearest tenth, and nearest hundredth.

19.

Decimal	Rounded to the Nearest		
	Whole Number	**Tenth**	**Hundredth**
2.768			
3.184			
0.476			
8.695			

Fill in the blanks.

20. A decimal rounded to the nearest tenth is 1.5.
Write two decimals that can be rounded to 1.5.

_____ and _____

21. A decimal rounded to the nearest hundredth is 4.26.
Write two decimals that can be rounded to 4.26.

_____ and _____

22. A decimal rounded to the nearest hundredth is 8.03.
The decimal is greater than 8.03.

What could this decimal be? _____

23. A decimal rounded to the nearest hundredth is 7.91.
The decimal is less than 7.91.

What could this decimal be? _____

Lesson 8.3 Rewriting Decimals as Fractions and Mixed Numbers

Rewrite each decimal as a fraction or mixed number in simplest form.

1.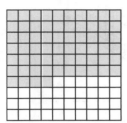

$0.64 = \dfrac{64}{100}$

$= $ _____

2.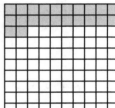

$1.22 = $ _____

3.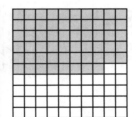

$2.58 = $ _____

4.

 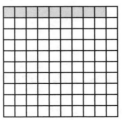

$3.09 = $ _____

5.

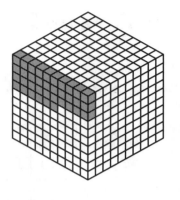

0.036 = _____

6.

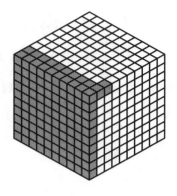

0.111 = _____

Rewrite each decimal as a fraction or mixed number in simplest form.

7.

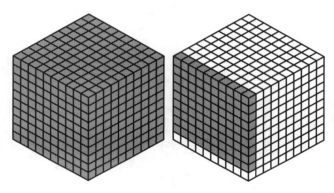

1.090 = _____

8.

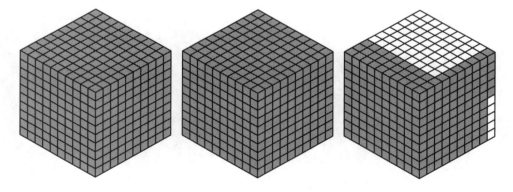

2.365 = _____

Rewrite each decimal as a fraction or mixed number in simplest form.

9.   2.64 = _____

10.   5.75 = _____

11.   7.008 = _____

12.   10.357 = _____

 Put on Your Thinking Cap!

Write your answer in the space given.

1. How many hundredths are there in 0.58? _____

2. How many hundredths are there in 2.09? _____

3. How many hundredths are there in 4.02? _____

4. How many thousandths are there in 2.067? _____

5. How many thousandths are there in 3.504? _____

6. How many thousandths are there in 0.953? _____

Round 16.997 to the nearest:

7. whole number _____

8. tenth _____

9. hundredth _____

Continue each number pattern.

10.

5.28, 5.58, 6.18, 7.08, 8.28, [ ]

+0.3   +0.6   +0.9   +1.2   +1.5

11.

1.25, 1.50, 2.00, 2.75, 3.75, [ ]

+0.25   +0.5   +0.75   +1.0   +1.25

12.

20.55, 20.3, 19.8, 19.05, 18.05, [ ]

−0.25   −0.5   −0.75   −1.0   −1.25

13.

1.5, 2.7, 4.7, 7.5, 11.1, [ ]

+1.2 +2.0 +2.8 +3.6 +4.4

+0.8 +0.8 +0.8 +0.8

14.

5.6, 7.4, 9.9, 13.1, 17.0, [ ]

+1.8 +2.5 +3.2 +3.9 +4.6

+0.7 +0.7 +0.7 +0.7

CHAPTER 9 Multiplying and Dividing Decimals

Lesson 9.1   Multiplying Decimals

Multiply. Write the product as a decimal.

1.   0.9 × 4 = _____ tenths × 4

= _____ tenths

= _____

2.   1.5 × 3 = _____ tenths × 3

= _____ tenths

= _____

3.   0.08 × 5 = _____ hundredths × 5

= _____ hundredths

= _____

4.   0.27 × 6 = _____ hundredths × 6

= _____ hundredths

= _____

5.   0.36 × 7 = _____ hundredths × 7

= _____ hundredths

= _____

Name: _____   Date: _____

Multiply.

6. $\begin{array}{r} 0.6 \\ \times\ \ \ 8 \\ \hline \end{array}$ **7.** $\begin{array}{r} 3.5 \\ \times\ \ \ 7 \\ \hline \end{array}$ **8.** $\begin{array}{r} 3.9 \\ \times\ \ \ 9 \\ \hline \end{array}$

9. $3 \times 8.7 =$ _____   **10.** $4 \times 6.9 =$ _____

11. $5 \times 7.4 =$ _____   **12.** $8 \times 9.2 =$ _____

13. $\begin{array}{r} 0.07 \\ \times\ \ \ \ 6 \\ \hline \end{array}$ **14.** $\begin{array}{r} 0.09 \\ \times\ \ \ \ 7 \\ \hline \end{array}$ **15.** $\begin{array}{r} 5.36 \\ \times\ \ \ \ 8 \\ \hline \end{array}$

16. $4 \times 7.04 =$ _____   **17.** $5 \times 4.58 =$ _____

18. $6 \times 5.64 =$ _____   **19.** $9 \times 8.36 =$ _____

Lesson 9.2 Multiplying by Tens, Hundreds, and Thousands

Multiply.

1. $4.85 \times 10 =$ _____

2. $0.375 \times 10 =$ _____

3. $4.928 \times 100 =$ _____

4. $0.23 \times 1,000 =$ _____

Complete.

5. $7.45 \times$ _____ $= 74.5$

6. _____ $\times 10 = 662.2$

7. $0.809 \times$ _____ $= 80.9$

8. _____ $\times 100 = 403$

9. $5.7 \times$ _____ $= 5,700$

10. _____ $\times 1,000 = 108$

Complete.

11. $513 = 51.3 \times$ _____

$= 5.13 \times$ _____

$= 0.513 \times$ _____

12. $4,016 =$ _____ $\times 10$

$=$ _____ $\times 100$

$=$ _____ $\times 1,000$

Complete.

13. $0.954 \times 60 = (0.954 \times$ _____ $) \times 10$

$=$ _____ $\times 10$

$=$ _____

14. $0.376 \times 800 = (0.376 \times$ _____ $) \times 100$

$=$ _____ $\times 100$

$=$ _____

Complete.

15. $0.97 \times 3{,}000 = (0.97 \times$ _____ $) \times 1{,}000$

                     $=$ _____ $\times 1{,}000$

                     $=$ _____

Find each product.

16. $1.25 \times 20 =$ _____   17. $2.8 \times 40 =$ _____

18. $15.9 \times 300 =$ _____   19 $7.286 \times 6{,}000 =$ _____

Solve. Show your work.

20.   There are 200 paperweights in a box. The mass of each paperweight is 0.085 kilogram. The mass of the empty box is 560 grams. What is the total mass of the box and 200 paperweights?

Lesson 9.3   Dividing Decimals

Complete. Write the quotient as a decimal.

1. $0.8 \div 2 = $ _____ tenths $\div 2$

$= $ _____ tenths

$= $ _____

2. $2.4 \div 4 = $ _____ tenths $\div 4$

$= $ _____ tenths

$= $ _____

3. $0.09 \div 3 = $ _____ hundredths $\div 3$

$= $ _____ hundredths

$= $ _____

4. $0.63 \div 7 = $ _____ hundredths $\div 7$

$= $ _____ hundredths

$= $ _____

5. $1.53 \div 9 = $ _____ hundredths $\div 9$

$= $ _____ hundredths

$= $ _____

Divide.

6. $4\overline{)9.2}$

7. $5\overline{)18.5}$

8. $8\overline{)25.6}$

9. $9\overline{)0.54}$

10. $3\overline{)33.99}$

11. $7\overline{)41.16}$

Divide.
Round each quotient to the nearest tenth.

12. $3.15 \div 4$

13. $4.17 \div 6$

Divide.
Round each quotient to the nearest hundredth.

14. $7.78 \div 3$

15. $14.59 \div 7$

Lesson 9.4   Dividing by Tens, Hundreds, and Thousands

Divide.

1. $2.36 \div 10 =$ _____

2. $30.15 \div 10 =$ _____

3. $508.2 \div 100 =$ _____

4. $210 \div 100 =$ _____

5. $780 \div 1,000 =$ _____

6. $82,300 \div 1,000 =$ _____

Complete.

7. $2.87 \div$ _____ $= 0.287$

8.   _____ $\div 10 = 34.5$

9. $319 \div$ _____ $= 3.19$

10.   _____ $\div 100 = 69.2$

11. $5,460 \div$ _____ $= 5.46$

12.   _____ $\div 1,000 = 48$

Complete.

13. $19.9 = 199 \div$ _____

$=$ _____ $\div 100$

$=$ _____ $\div 1,000$

14. $8.235 =$ _____ $\div 10$

$= 823.5 \div$ _____

$= 8,235 \div$ _____

15. $4.01 =$ _____ $\div 10$

$=$ _____ $\div 100$

$=$ _____ $\div 1,000$

16. $67.67 = 676.7 \div$ _____

$= 6,767 \div$ _____

$= 67,670 \div$ _____

Complete.

17. $298 ÷ 20 = (298 ÷$ _____ $) ÷ 10$

$=$ _____ $÷ 10$

$=$ _____

18. $32 ÷ 800 = (32 ÷$ _____ $) ÷ 100$

$=$ _____ $÷ 100$

$=$ _____

19. $1{,}200 ÷ 6{,}000 = (1{,}200 ÷$ _____ $) ÷ 1{,}000$

$=$ _____ $÷ 1{,}000$

$=$ _____

Divide.

20. $450 ÷ 60 =$ _____

21. $64.8 ÷ 80 =$ _____

22. $36.8 ÷ 400 =$ _____

23. $576 ÷ 900 =$ _____

24. $1{,}050 ÷ 3{,}000 =$ _____

25. $8{,}320 ÷ 4{,}000 =$ _____

Solve. Show your work.

26. Susan pours 125 liters of apple juice into 500 cups equally. How many liters of apple juice are in each cup?

27. A 370-meter roll of string is cut into 2,000 pieces that are all the same length. Find the length of each cut piece of string.

28.   Mr. Jones bought 30 files and some books. He paid $97.50 for the files. Each book cost 10 times as much as a file. What was the cost of each book?

29.   Jane bought 10 pears and 11 oranges for $10.05. The total cost of 1 pear and 1 orange was $0.94. How much did 1 orange cost?

Lesson 9.5   Estimating Decimals

**Round each decimal to the nearest whole number.
Then estimate the result.**

1. $9.99 + $5.99

2. $49.50 + $19.65

3. $99.59 − $19.95

4. $89.90 − $20.25

5.   9.9 × 4.6

6.   39.7 × 7.6

7.   9.4 × 30.3

8.   34.8 ÷ 5.4

9.   87.7 ÷ 7.8

10.   96.49 ÷ 3.9

**Round each number to the nearest tenth.
Then estimate the result.**

11.   9.48 km + 13.63 km

12.   8.07 kg − 3.79 kg

13.   7.56 kg × 9

14.   9.64 L ÷ 8

Solve. Show your work.

15.   Each tin of biscuits is sold for $4.95. Estimate the cost of 4 tins of biscuits.

16.   Vivien's handspan measures 18.5 centimeters. Estimate the number of times Vivien uses her handspan to measure a length of 1 meter 75 centimeters.

Lesson 9.6   Real-World Problems: Decimals

Solve. Show your work.

1. Each bottle contains 1.25 liters of orange juice. How many liters of orange juice are there in 8 bottles?

2. Keith thinks of a number. When he multiples the number by 6 and subtracts 19.85 from the product, he gets 29.77. Find the number.

3. An ice cream stand is 1.38 kilometers from the starting point of a bike path. Brian rides his bike from the starting point to the ice cream stand and back to the starting point 3 times. How many kilometers does Brian ride his bike?

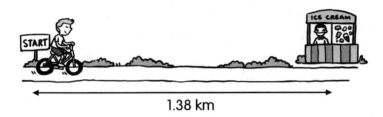

1.38 km

4. A bottle contains 0.85 liter of concentrated orange juice. Teresa adds 9 times as much water to the orange concentrate in the bottle to make drinks for her party.

  a. How much water does Teresa add?

  b. The capacity of each cup is 250 milliliters. How many full cups of juice can Teresa make?

5. The cost of 4 identical pencils is $1.90. Find the cost of 14 of these pencils.

6. The mass of a container is 5.81 kilograms when completely filled with sugar. The mass of the container is 3.8 kilograms when $\frac{3}{8}$ of the sugar is removed. What is the mass of the empty container?

7. At the deli, 100 grams of ham cost $1.50 and 100 grams of sausages cost $0.85 more than the ham. Paul buys 1.2 kilograms of ham and 600 grams of sausages. How much does Paul pay?

8. Regina had 30 meters of ribbon. She gave 2.7 meters of the ribbon to each of her four friends and used the rest to tie some presents for her birthday party. Each present required 75 centimeters of ribbon to tie. Find the maximum number of presents Regina could tie.

9.   Maria wants to shop at Simon's Bakery. She needs to buy 100 fruitcakes for her birthday party. How much will Maria need to spend?

SIMON'S BAKERY

1 fruitcake: $1.50
2 fruitcakes FREE for every
10 fruitcakes bought

10.   The admission fee for an exhibition is $8.50 for each adult and $3.50 for each child. On Friday, a total of $5,120 was collected. 160 more children than adults visited the exhibition. How many children visited the exhibition on Friday?

11. The total mass of a box and 3 identical tennis balls is 1.02 kilograms. When the number of tennis balls in the box is tripled, the total mass becomes 2.16 kilograms. What is the mass, in kilograms, of the empty box?

12. The table shows the cost of shrimp at three stalls:

	Joe's Stall	Paul's Stall	Sam's Stall
Price of Shrimp	$19.00 per kg	$2.20 per 100 g	$11.00 for 0.5 kg

a. Which two stalls sell shrimp at the same price? How much do they sell 1 kilogram of shrimp for?

b. How much money would you save if you bought 2.5 kilograms of shrimp from the least expensive stall instead of from the stalls in part A?

Name: _____ **Date:** _____

13. Mark and Carlos started saving money at the same time. Mark saved $1.20 daily and Carlos saved $0.30 more than Mark each day. How much did Mark save if Carlos saved a total of $11.40 more than Mark?

14. Fiona bought some oranges and 8 mangoes for a total of $30.80. For every mango Fiona bought, she could buy 4 oranges with the same amount of money. A mango cost $2.10 more than an orange.

a. What was the cost of each type of fruit?

b. Express the number of oranges bought as a fraction of the total number of fruits bought.

15.   Mrs. Belen wanted to bake 10 loaves of bread but realized she needed 1.75 kilograms more of flour. If she baked 7 loaves of bread, she would have 0.5 kilogram of flour left.

    a.   How much flour was needed for each loaf of bread?

    b.   Each kilogram of flour cost $0.90. How much would Mrs. Belen pay for all of the flour she needed to bake 10 loaves of bread?

 Put on Your Thinking Cap!

Solve. Show your work.

1. A pile of 12 books is 1.2 meters thick. 9 of them are 9.5 centimeters thick each and the rest are of equal thickness. For the rest of the books, how thick is each of them in centimeters?

2. Charles and his 5 siblings buy a present for their mother on Mother's Day. As the eldest brother, Charles pays 0.2 of the cost of the present. The rest of his siblings pay the balance equally. Each sibling pays $9.50 less than Charles. What is the cost of the present?

3. The total capacity of 1 carton is the same as the total capacity of 2 identical cups. If 1.8 liters of water are needed to fill up 3 identical cups and 2 identical cartons, what is the capacity of a cup? Express your answer correct to 2 decimal places.

4. The total mass of 4 cartons of milk and 7 bottles of apple juice is 2.38 kilograms. The total mass of 2 cartons of milk and 3 bottles of apple juice is 1.1 kilograms. Find the mass of a carton of milk. Give your answer in kilograms.

5. At a cafe, Paul paid $12.50 for 2 cups of coffee and 2 cups of tea. The cost of each cup of tea was $\frac{2}{3}$ the cost of each cup of coffee.

  a. How much did each cup of coffee cost?

  b. How much did Paul's friend, Leon, pay for 2 cups of coffee and 1 cup of tea?

6. The mass of a can of orange juice is 0.16 kilogram heavier than the mass of a can of mango juice. The mass of 6 cans of orange juice is the same as the mass of 9 cans of mango juice.

  a. What is the mass of each can of mango juice?

  b. What is the mass of each can of orange juice?

7. Kerrie bought 5 notebooks and 5 pens. Devon bought 8 notebooks and 4 pens. They both paid the same amount. Each notebook cost $3.70 less than the cost of each pen.

    a. What was the cost of each notebook?

    b. What was the cost of each pen?

8. At a cafe, each chicken sandwich costs 0.8 times as much as each cheese sandwich. Daniel pays $46.15 for 9 chicken sandwiches and 7 cheese sandwiches.

    a. What is the cost of each chicken sandwich?

    b. What is the cost of each cheese sandwich?

9. James was given some alarm clocks and 30 patches to sell during a charity fund raising project. He was supposed to sell each alarm clock for $15.50 and each patch for $2.30. Instead, James worked out a plan in order to avoid accepting coins. He sold each clock for $16 and each patch for $2. James collected the same amount of money using the new prices as he would have with the old prices. How many alarm clocks did James sell?

10. Sarah saves $1.50 daily while Jessica saves $1 more than Sarah each day.
     Although Jessica started saving 10 days later than Sarah, she has now saved
     $12 more than Sarah.
     a.   How many days has Sarah been saving?

     b.   How much money has Jessica saved so far?

11. Albert went shopping with half of his monthly allowance. He spent $35.50 on a shirt and $\frac{3}{5}$ of the remainder on a book. He had $25.80 left after his shopping trip. What was Albert's monthly allowance?

© 2009 Marshall Cavendish International (Singapore) Private Limited. Copying is permitted; see page ii.

12. Regina paid $12.50 for 4 chicken sandwiches and 3 apple pies. The cost of each apple pie was 0.75 the cost of each chicken sandwich. How much did each chicken sandwich cost?

Percent

Lesson 10.1   Percent

Write each item as a fraction, decimal, or percent.

	Fraction	Decimal	Percentage
1.	$\frac{5}{10}$		
2.	$\frac{25}{100}$		
3.	$\frac{20}{100}$		
4.		0.3	
5.		0.45	
6.		0.32	
7.			75%
8.			60%
9.			15%

Solve. Show your work.

10.   During a math quiz, students had to complete
      100 questions. Jerry completed only 84 questions.
      a.   What percent of the questions were not completed by Jerry?

      b.   What fraction of the questions did Jerry complete?

11.   In the gym, $\frac{36}{100}$ of the students are girls. What percent of the students
      in the gym are boys?

Lesson 10.2   Expressing Fractions as Percents

Express each fraction as a percent.

1. $\dfrac{1}{2}$ = _____ %	**2.** $\dfrac{1}{4}$ = _____ %
3. $\dfrac{2}{5}$ = _____ %	**4.** $\dfrac{3}{8}$ = _____ %
5. $\dfrac{5}{8}$ = _____ %	**6.** $\dfrac{11}{20}$ = _____ %
7. $\dfrac{16}{25}$ = _____ %	**8.** $\dfrac{37}{50}$ = _____ %
9. $\dfrac{72}{300}$ = _____ %	**10.** $\dfrac{184}{400}$ = _____ %
11. $\dfrac{270}{300}$ = _____ %	**12.** $\dfrac{440}{500}$ = _____ %

Solve. Show your work.

13. There were 300 participants in an art competition.
Of the participants, 240 completed their drawings.
What percent of the participants did not complete their drawings?

14. There are 250 blue and yellow beads in a box.
There are 60 fewer yellow beads than blue beads in the box.
What percent of the beads in the box are yellow?

15. After spending $6.75 on a meal and $1.25 on drinks, Maria had $12 left.
What percent of her money did Maria spend?

16. There are two sizes of red and blue marbles in a box. Of the big marbles in
the box, 45 are red and $\frac{3}{4}$ are blue. The fraction of small marbles that are red
is $\frac{2}{5}$ and the fraction of small marbles that are blue is $\frac{3}{5}$. There are 24 more
small blue marbles than small red marbles. What percent of the marbles are
big marbles?

17. Glen collects a total of 450 stamps from the United States, Great Britain, and India. In his collection, 52% of the stamps are U.S. stamps. He has $\frac{3}{5}$ as many Indian stamps as British stamps.

a. How many Indian stamps does Glen have?

b. What percent of Glen's collection are British stamps?

18. Mr. Smith baked 144 blueberry pies, some strawberry pies, and some apple pies. The number of apple pies is $\frac{4}{5}$ of the number of strawberry pies. There are 24 more strawberry pies than apple pies. What percent of the pies are blueberry pies?

Lesson 10.3   Percent of a Number

Multiply.

1. 25% of $360		**2.** 75% of 24 hours	
3. 60% of 160 km		**4.** 80% of 5,600 people	
5. 45% of 8 kg		**6.** 30% of 2 L 370 mL	

Solve. Show your work.

7. Of the 480 flowers in a shop, 30% are lilies, 45% are orchids, and the rest are roses. How many roses are there in the shop?

8. Of the 350 students in a hall, 20% are girls. Then, 50 more girls entered the hall. Now, what percent of students in the hall are girls?

Lesson 10.4   Real-World Problems: Percent

Solve. Show your work.

1. Leon deposited $30,000 in a bank which paid 2% interest per year. After 1 year, Leon withdrew all his money including the interest. How much money did Leon withdraw in all?

2. At a flower shop, 4 flowers cost $10. Mrs. Watson usually buys 12 flowers. During a sale, there is a 20% discount on every flower. How many flowers can Mrs. Watson buy during the sale if she spends the same amount of money that she usually does?

3.   Peter's allowance is the same every month. Each month Peter spends $114 and saves the rest. He saves $432 in a year. What percent of his allowance does Peter save every month?

4.   Cheryl used 40% of her money to buy a dress and $\frac{1}{5}$ of the remainder to buy a pair of shoes. She then donated $60 to charity and had $132 left. How much money did Cheryl have at first?

Put on Your Thinking Cap!

Solve. Show your work.

1. Mrs. Li bought some crackers. She gave 30% of the crackers to her neighbor and ate 50% of the remaining crackers. Mrs. Li had 42 crackers left. How many crackers did Mrs. Li buy?

2. In the eco-garden of a school, the number of aquatic animals is 80% of the number of aquatic plants. There are 162 aquatic plants and animals in all. How many aquatic animals are there in the eco-garden?

3. Of the 150 goldfish that Joanna bought, 60% were females and the rest were males. When some female goldfish died, the percent of female goldfish became 52%.

   a. How many male goldfish were there?

   b. How many female goldfish died?

4. Of the 280 muffins that Mr. Parker baked, 40% were corn muffins. How many more corn muffins must Mr. Parker bake so that 60% of the muffins are corn muffins?

Name: _____   **Date:** _____

Test Prep

50

for Chapters 8 to 10

Multiple Choice   (10 × 2 points = 20 points)

Fill in the circle next to the correct answer.

1.   Round 5.995 to the nearest hundredth.

Ⓐ 5.99   Ⓑ 5.90   Ⓒ 6.10   Ⓓ 6.00

2.   Express $\frac{7}{8}$ as a percent.

Ⓐ 68%   Ⓑ 78.5%   Ⓒ 87.5%   Ⓓ 88%

3.   The mass of a watermelon is 2.4 kilograms and the mass of a pineapple is 0.75 kilogram less than the watermelon. Find the total mass of the fruits.

Ⓐ 1.65 kg   Ⓑ 3.15 kg   Ⓒ 4.05 kg   Ⓓ 5.55 kg

4.   Matthew pours 150 liters of apple juice equally into 600 cups. How many liters of apple juice are in each cup?

Ⓐ 0.20 L   Ⓑ 0.25 L   Ⓒ 0.35 L   Ⓓ 0.45 L

5.   In order to fill the bucket, 50 identical bottles are needed. The capacity of each bottle is 0.75 liter. What is the capacity of the bucket?

Ⓐ 36.25 L   Ⓑ 36.5 L   Ⓒ 37.25 L   Ⓓ 37.5 L

6. Mr. Thomas pays $190 for 200 keychains. How much does each keychain cost?

(A) $0.75   (B) $0.85   (C) $0.95   (D) $1.05

7. The cost of 4 identical pens is $8.20. Find the cost of 7 of these pens.

(A) $2.05   (B) $2.50   (C) $14.35   (D) $17.50

8. There were 40 questions on the test. Rebecca answered 28 questions correctly. What percent of the questions did Rebecca answer correctly?

(A) 30%   (B) 40%   (C) 60%   (D) 70%

9. There are 90 dogs and 60 hamsters in a pet shop. What percent of the animals in the pet shop are dogs?

(A) 40%   (B) 50%   (C) 60%   (D) 66.7%

10. There are 180 beads in a box. Of the beads in the box, 40% are red beads and the rest are white beads. How many white beads are in the box?

(A) 108   (B) 72   (C) 45   (D) 30

Name: _____   **Date:** _____

Short Answer (10 × 2 points = 20 points)

Write your answer in the space given.

11.   Express 7.25 as a mixed number in simplest form.

Answer: _____

12.   Express $6\frac{17}{20}$ as a decimal.

Answer: _____

13. $3.75 + 1.25 - \boxed{} = 2.35$
What is the missing decimal?

Answer: _____

14.   8 tenths + 76 hundredths = _____.
Give your answer as a decimal.

Answer: _____

15.   The cost of 100 grams of cashews is $0.75. Betty buys 3 kilograms of cashews. How much does Betty pay?

Answer: $_____

16. Chicken eggs cost $2.40 for 10 eggs. Duck eggs cost $1.14 for 6 eggs. Find the difference in the price of one chicken egg and one duck egg.

Answer: _____¢

17. Ahmed scored 75 points on his English test, 72 points on his math test, and 71 points on his science test. Find Ahmed's average score for his tests. Round your answer to the nearest whole number.

Answer: _____

18. Ivy is 9 years old. Her age is 25% of her mother's age. Express Ivy's age as a percent of her mother's age 9 years from now.

Answer: _____%

19. There are 300 students in Grade 5. On a mid-year exam, 20% of the students scored an A and 45% of the remainder scored a B. How many students scored a B in the exam?

Answer: _____

20. Of the participants in a survey, $\frac{2}{5}$ are girls, 5% are adults, and the rest are boys. There are 270 more boys than girls in the survey. How many adults participated in the survey?

Answer: _____

Extended Response (Questions 21 and 22: 2 × 3 points, Question 23: 4 points)

Solve. Show your work.

21. A badminton racket costs $\frac{4}{5}$ the cost of a tennis racket. The tennis racket costs $7.60 more than the badminton racket. What is the cost of the badminton racket?

22. Of the fruits in a basket, 48% are mangoes and the rest are apples and pears. The number of pears is $\frac{5}{8}$ of the number of apples. There are 128 more mangoes than apples. How many pears are in the basket?

23. Of the 160 pies that Jack baked, 55% were apple pies and the rest were cherry pies. After Jack sold some of the apple pies, the percent of apple pies became 40%.

   a. How many pies were left?

   b. How many apple pies were sold?

© 2009 Marshall Cavendish International (Singapore) Private Limited. Copying is permitted; see page ii.

CHAPTER 11 Graphs and Probability

Lesson 11.1   Making and Interpreting Double Bar Graphs

The double bar graph shows the number of students in five schools who obtained the gold and silver awards in a physical fitness test. Use the graph for the following exercises.

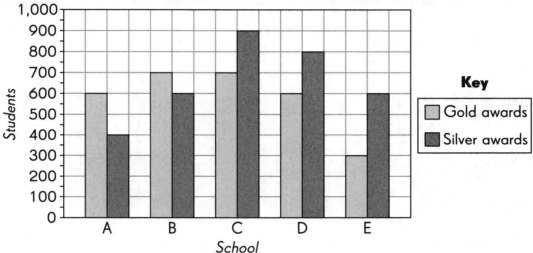

Students who Obtained Gold and Silver Awards

Key
Gold awards
Silver awards

1. _____ students participated in the physical fitness test in School B.

2. There are _____ more students who obtained the gold award in School C than in School E.

3. The fraction of the number of students in School E who obtained the gold award out of its total number of students that obtained either gold or silver awards is _____.

4. _____ percent of the students receiving awards in School A obtained the gold award.

5. The ratio of the number of students who obtained the silver award in School A to School B to School D is _____.

Complete the bar graph using the data in the table. Then use the graph for the following exercises.

6. The table shows the product sales for a company during the first five months of the year.

	January	February	March	April	May
Product 1	60	30	50	70	40
Product 2	90	50	70	110	80

7. The average amount of Product 1 sold during the first five months

    is _____.

8. The ratio of the amount of Product 1 sold in January to the amount of

    Product 1 sold in May is _____.

9. The month of _____ shows the greatest decrease in sales of Product 2.

    The decrease was _____.

10. _____ percent of the total sales for Product 2 was sold in May.

Lesson 11.2   Graphing an Equation

Name the coordinates of the given points.

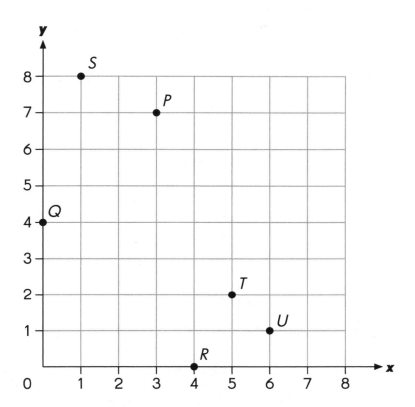

1.   P   _____

2.   Q   _____

3.   R   _____

4.   S   _____

5.   T   _____

6.   U   _____

Plot and label each point on the graph.

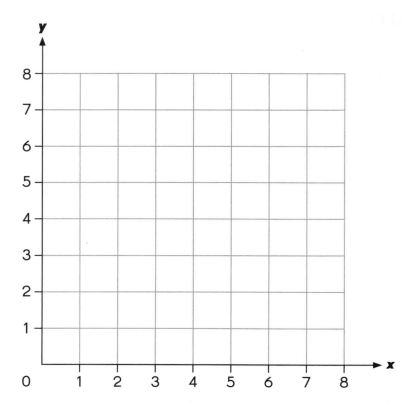

7.   *A* (0, 6)   **8.**   *B* (5, 1)

9.   *C* (3, 3)   **10.**   *D* (7, 0)

11.   *E* (4, 8)   **12.**   *F* (6, 2)

Name: _____   Date: _____

● **One yard (Y) is 3 times the length of one foot (F). This information can be represented by the graph Y = 3F.**

A graph of Y = 3F is drawn.

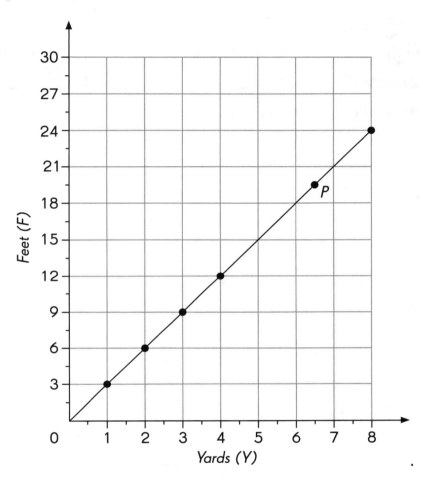

How many feet are there in:

13.   3 yards = _____

14. $5\frac{1}{2}$ yards = _____

How many yards are there in:

15.   12 feet = _____

16.   21 feet = _____

17.   What are the values at the point *P*?

Yards = _____   Feet = _____

The length of a rectangle is twice its width. This information can be represented by the graph L = 2W.

18.   Complete the following table.

Width (W) inch	1	2		5		8
Length (L = 2W) inch	2	4	8		12	

Complete the line graph using the data in the table.

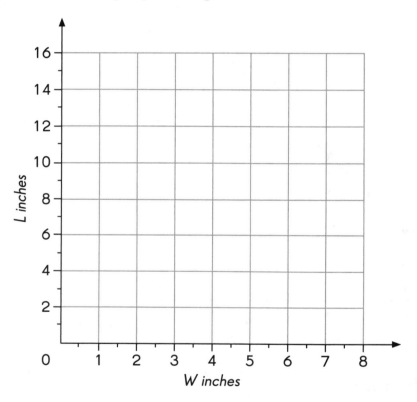

W inches

Find the length of the rectangle in these exercises:

19.   The width of the rectangle is 3 inches. The length is _____ inches.

20.   The width of the rectangle is 5.5 inches. The length is _____ inches.

Find the width of the rectangle in these exercises:

21.   The length of the rectangle is 6 inches. The width is _____ inches.

22.   The length of the rectangle is 14 inches. The width is _____ inches.

Lesson 11.3   Combinations

Solve. Show your work.

1.   Mrs. Johnson bakes some pies in 3 different sizes: small, medium, and large. She uses 4 different kinds of filling: fish, beef, chicken, and mushroom. How many different pies can she bake?

2.   Mr. Samuel has a few options to consider before deciding what type of car to purchase:

   2 functions: Manual or automatic.
   2 capacities: 1,600 cc or 2,000 cc.
   3 colors: Blue, white, or grey.

   How many combinations of options does Mr. Samuel need to consider?

3. Ms. Beckham invites 5 friends to her birthday party. How many handshakes are there if each person at the party shakes hands with every other person at the party?

4. A restaurant is having a special promotion for a three-course meal. Diners are allowed to choose one dish from each of the three lists below.

Soups	**Main Meals**	**Desserts**
Mixed vegetable (V)	Steak & chips (S)	Mixed fruits (F)
Chicken & Corn (C)	Fish & chips (F)	Apple pie (A)
Mushroom (M)	Lamb chops (L)	Ice cream (I)

How many three-course meal combinations does the restaurant offer?
Make a list of all the combinations.

Lesson 11.4 Theoretical Probability and Experimental Probability

Determine the experimental probability of an outcome.

You need a bag and 4 counters of different colors: red, blue, green, and yellow.

Step 1 Place the counters in the bag. Make a guess about which color counter you will pull out of the bag.

Step 2 Shake the bag and take a counter from the bag without looking.

Step 3 If the counter matches your guess, put a check in the table.

Step 4 If the counter does not match your guess, put an **X** in the table.

Step 5 Place the counter on the table.

Step 6 Repeat Steps 1 through 5 until you have removed all four counters from the bag.

Step 7 Repeat the experiment 10 times.

Guess			
1st	2nd	3rd	4th

Use the data in the table. Give your answer as a whole number or fraction.

1. What is the experimental probability of being correct on the first guess?

_____

2. What is the experimental probability of being correct on the last guess?

_____

Use the data in the table on page 69. Give your answer as a whole number or fraction.

3.   What is the theoretical probability of being correct on the first guess?

_____

4.   What is the theoretical probability of being correct on the second guess?

_____

Compare the results of an experiment with the theoretical probability.

You need two number cubes, numbered 1 through 6, for this experiment.

Step 1   Roll both cubes.

Step 2   Add the two numbers.

Step 3   Record the sum in the table by shading the squares in the correct row.

Step 4   Repeat this process 15 times.

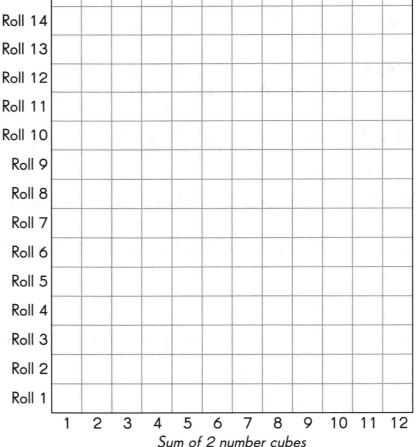

Experiment

Sum of 2 number cubes

● **Fill in the blanks.**

5. Which total sum occurred most often? _____

6. What is the experimental probability of rolling the sum that occurred most

often? _____

7. Which total score occurred least often? _____

8. What is the experimental probability of rolling the sum that occurred least

often? _____

9. What is the experimental probability of rolling a sum of 10? _____

● **10.** Complete the table to show the possible sums when rolling the two number
cubes.

1st cube

+	1	2	3	4	5	6
1						7
2					7	
3				7		
4			7			
5		7				
6	7					

2nd cube (label to the left of the row headers)

Use the data in the table on page 71. Fill in the blanks.

11. Which sum can occur most often? _____

Is this theoretical probability the same as your experimental probability from Exercise 6? (Yes or No) _____

12. Which sum can occur least often? _____

Is this theoretical probability the same as your experimental probability from Exercise 8? (Yes or No) _____

13. What is the theoretical probability of rolling a sum of 8? _____

A spinner is divided into four equal colored sections: red, yellow, green, and blue. The spinner has a pointer which, when spun, comes to rest in any one of the four sections.

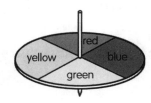

The spinner was spun 80 times and the results were recorded in the table.

Outcome	Red	Yellow	Green	Blue
Number of Times	18	16	24	22

Use the data in the table. Give your answer as a fraction.

14. The experimental probability of landing on red is _____.

15. The experimental probability of landing on yellow is _____.

16. The experimental probability of landing on green is _____.

17. The experimental probability of landing on blue is _____.

18. The theoretical probability of landing on any one of the four colors is _____.

Put on Your Thinking Cap!

Create a double bar graph.
Follow the steps.
You will need a small ball and a few friends to take part in the experiment.

Step 1   Toss the ball to each friend 8 times. Make sure that your friends use their right hands to catch the ball.

Step 2   Toss the ball to each friend 8 more times. Make sure that your friends use their left hands to catch the ball.

Step 3   Count the number of catches. Record the results in the table below.

Name	Right-hand Catches	Left-hand Catches

Step 4   Draw a double bar graph of the results.

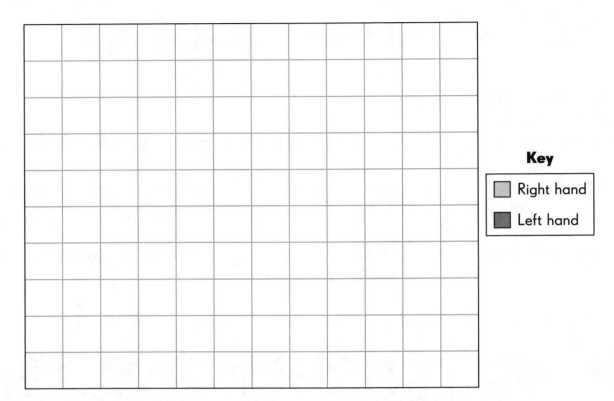

Key

Right hand

Left hand

1.   Who caught the most balls?

_____

2.   Which hand is better suited for catching the ball?
Give a reason for this result.

_____

_____

_____

_____

Angles

Lesson 12.1   Angles on a Line

Find the unknown marked angles. The diagrams are not drawn to scale.

1. $\overleftrightarrow{AC}$ is a line. Find the measure of $\angle DBE$.

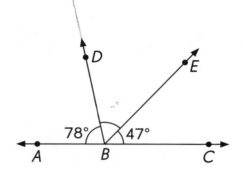

2. $\overleftrightarrow{PR}$ is a line. Find the measure of $\angle PQT$.

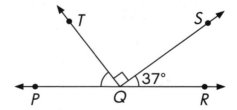

3. $\overleftrightarrow{CE}$ is a line. Find the measure of $\angle FDG$.

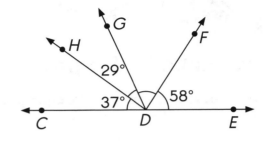

4. $\overleftrightarrow{SU}$ is a line. The measure of $\angle y$ is twice as big as the measure of $\angle x$ and the measure of $\angle z$ is half the measure of a right angle. Find the measure of $\angle y$.

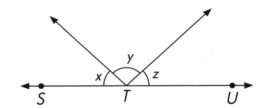

Lesson 12.2   Angles at a Point

Find the unknown marked angles. The diagrams are not drawn to scale.

1. Find the measure of ∠a.

2. Find the measure of ∠b.

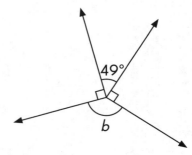

3. $\overleftrightarrow{AB}$ and $\overleftrightarrow{CD}$ meet at O. Find the measure of $\angle c$.

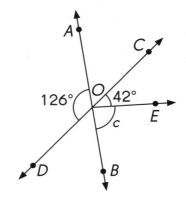

4. $\overleftrightarrow{AB}$ is a line. The measure of $\angle e$ is 2 times the measure of $\angle d$. Find the measures of $\angle d$ and $\angle e$.

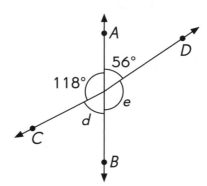

Lesson 12.3   Vertical Angles

Find the unknown marked angles. The diagrams are not drawn to scale.

1. $\overleftrightarrow{AB}$, $\overleftrightarrow{CD}$, and $\overleftrightarrow{EF}$ meet at G. Find the measure of $\angle DGE$.

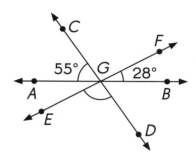

2. $\overleftrightarrow{AB}$, $\overleftrightarrow{CD}$, $\overleftrightarrow{EF}$, and $\overleftrightarrow{GH}$ meet at O. Find the measure of $\angle EOH$.

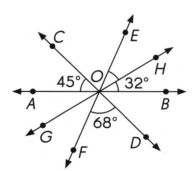

3. $\overleftrightarrow{AB}$ and $\overleftrightarrow{CD}$ meet at E and $\overrightarrow{EF}$ is perpendicular to $\overleftrightarrow{CD}$. Find the measure of $\angle AEF$.

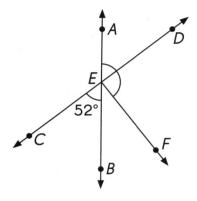

4. $\overleftrightarrow{AB}$ and $\overleftrightarrow{CD}$ meet at O. Find the measure of $\angle BOE$.

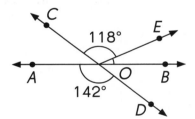

5.   Look at the marked angles in the diagram. In the table below, write all sets of:

a.   angles at a point,

b.   vertical angles, and

c.   angles on a line

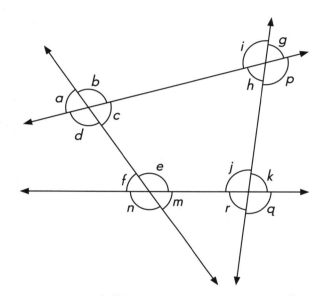

Angles at a Point	Vertical Angles	Angles on a Line
∠a, ∠b, ∠c, and ∠d	∠b and ∠d	∠b and ∠c

Find the unknown marked angles. The diagrams are not drawn to scale.

6.   *ABCD* is a square. The measure of ∠*ADE* is 42°. Find the measure of ∠*EDF.*

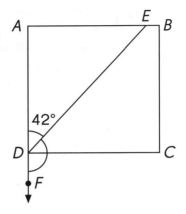

7. $\overleftrightarrow{DF}$ is a line and $\overrightarrow{OA}$ is perpendicular to $\overrightarrow{OB}$.
Find the measure of ∠*COE*.

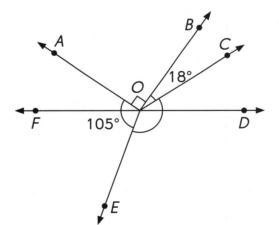

 **Put on Your Thinking Cap!**

Find the measures of the unknown angles.

1. $\overleftrightarrow{AB}$ and $\overleftrightarrow{EF}$ meet at D. $\overrightarrow{DC}$ is perpendicular to $\overleftrightarrow{AB}$ and $\overrightarrow{DG}$ is perpendicular to $\overleftrightarrow{EF}$. Find the measure of $\angle x$.

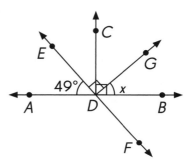

2. In the diagram, the sum of $\angle x$ and $\angle y$ is 124°, the sum of $\angle y$ and $\angle z$ is 142°, and the sum of $\angle x$ and $\angle z$ is 94°. Find the measures of $\angle x$, $\angle y$, and $\angle z$.

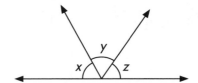

3.   In the diagram, the ratio of the measures of ∠x to ∠y is 3 : 4.
The measure of ∠x is 51°.
Find the measure of ∠z.

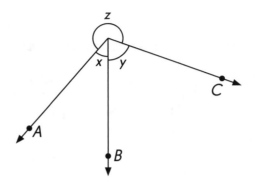

4. $\overleftrightarrow{AB}$ and $\overleftrightarrow{CD}$ meet at G. The ratio of the measures of ∠x to ∠y is 5 : 2.
Find the measure of ∠z.

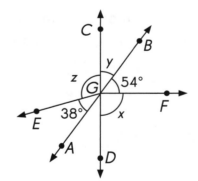

5. In the diagram, the measure of $\angle p$ is 7 times the measure of $\angle q$ and the measure of $\angle r$ is 4 times the measure of $\angle q$.
Find the measures of $\angle p$ and $\angle r$.

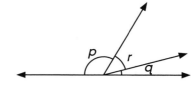

6. In the diagram, the measures of $\angle a$, $\angle b$, and $\angle c$ are in the ratio $3 : 4 : 5$.
Find the measures of $\angle a$, $\angle b$, and $\angle c$.

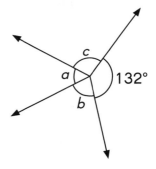

7.   In the diagram, $\angle c$ lies on a line. The measure of $\angle a$ is $\frac{2}{3}$ of $\angle d$, the measure of $\angle d$ is $\frac{3}{4}$ of $\angle b$, and the measure $\angle b$ is $\frac{4}{9}$ of $\angle c$. Find the measures of $\angle a$, $\angle b$, $\angle c$, and $\angle d$.

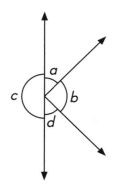

8. $\overleftrightarrow{AF}$ is a line. $\angle AOB$ and $\angle COD$ are right angles. The measure of $\angle EOC$ is 130° and the measure of $\angle EOF$ is 108°. What can you say about the measures of $\angle BOC$ and $\angle DOF$?

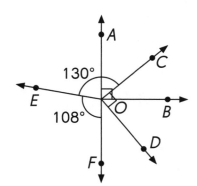

CHAPTER 13 Properties of Triangles and Four-Sided Figures

Lesson 13.1 Classifying Triangles

1. Classify the following triangles by sides as a scalene triangle, an isosceles triangle, or an equilateral triangle.

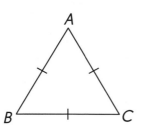

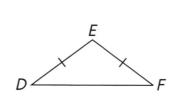

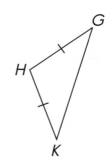

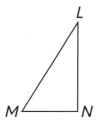

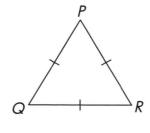

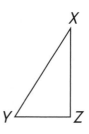

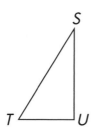

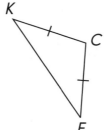

Scalene Triangles	Equilateral Triangles	Isosceles Triangles

2. Classify the following triangles by angles as a right triangle, an isosceles triangle, or an equilateral triangle. Use a protractor to help you classify the triangles.

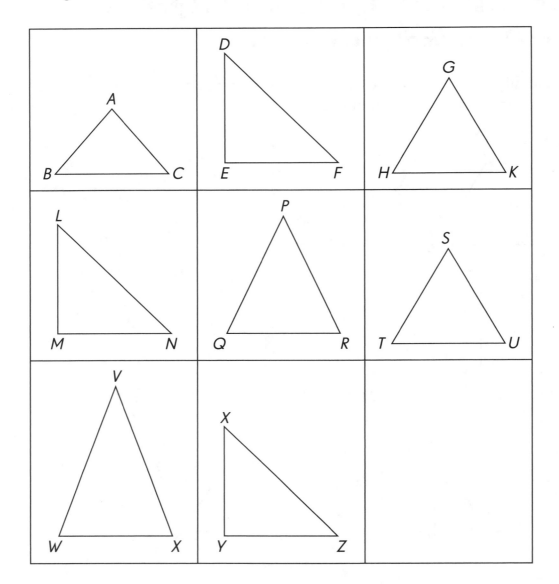

Right Triangles	Equilateral Triangles	Isosceles Triangles

Lesson 13.2   Measures of Angles of a Triangle

Find the unknown angle measures. The figures are not drawn to scale.

1.

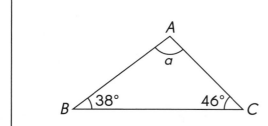

$m\angle a =$

2.

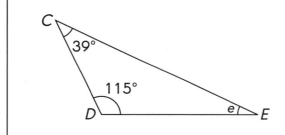

$m\angle e =$

3.

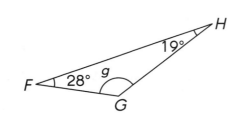

$m\angle g =$

4.

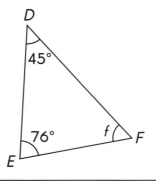

$m\angle f =$

5.

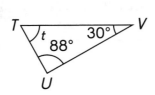

m∠t =

6.

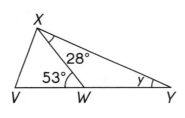

m∠r =

7.

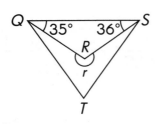

m∠y =

8.

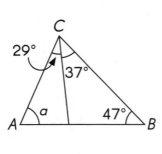

m∠a =

Lesson 13.3   Right, Isosceles, and Equilateral Triangles

Find the unknown angle measures in each right triangle. The figures are not drawn to scale.

1.   *ABC* is a right triangle.
Find the measure of ∠*ACB*.

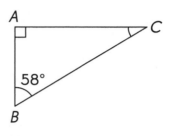

2.   *PQR* is a right triangle.
Find the measure of ∠*PRQ*.

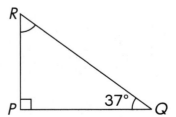

Find the unknown angle measures. The figures are not drawn to scale.

3.   *ABC* is a right triangle.
        Find the measure of ∠*BCD*.

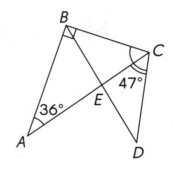

4.   *EBD* is an isosceles triangle with *ED* = *EB*, m∠*BEC* = 34°, and m∠*CBD* = 44°.
        Find the measure of ∠*EBC*.

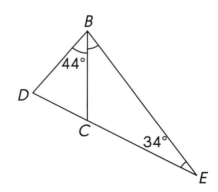

Find the unknown angle measures in each figure. The figures are not drawn to scale.

5.   *AOB* is an isosceles triangle. *OA = OB*.
        AOC is a right triangle.
        Find the measure of ∠*OCB*

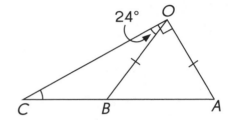

6.   *ABC* is an equilateral triangle and *ACD* is an isosceles triangle.
        Find the measure of ∠*ADC*.

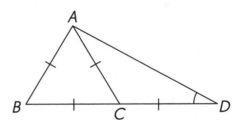

7. *ABCDEF* is a 6-sided figure. All the triangles are equilateral triangles. Find the measure of ∠*FAB*.

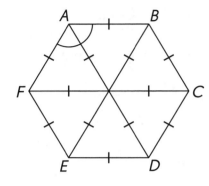

8. *ABC* is an equilateral triangle. *BA* = *BD*. Find the measure of ∠*AEC*.

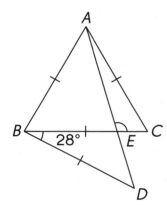

Lesson 13.4   Triangle Inequalities

Complete. Measure the sides of the triangle to the nearest inch.

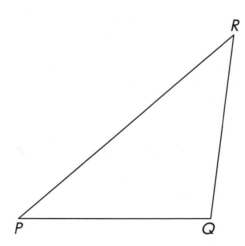

1. $PQ =$ _____ in. $QR =$ _____ in. $PR =$ _____ in.

2. $PQ + QR =$ _____ in.

3. $PQ + PR =$ _____ in.

4. $PR + QR =$ _____ in.

Use your answers in Exercises 1 to 4. Fill in the blanks with *Yes* or *No*.

5.   Is $PQ + QR > PR$?   _____

6.   Is $PQ + PR > QR$?   _____

7.   Is $PR + QR > PQ$?   _____

Complete. Measure the sides of the triangle to the nearest centimeter.

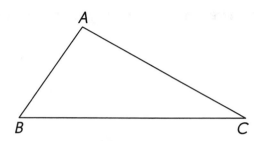

8. $BC =$ _____ cm $AB =$ _____ cm $AC =$ _____ cm

9. $AB + BC =$ _____ cm

10. $AB + AC =$ _____ cm

11. $BC + AC =$ _____ cm

Use your answers in Exercises 8 to 11. Write the sides of the triangle to make the inequalities true.

12. $AB + BC >$ _____

13. $AB + AC >$ _____

14. $BC + AC >$ _____

● **The lengths of two sides of each triangle are given. Name a possible length for the third side. The given lengths are in whole centimeters or inches.**

15.

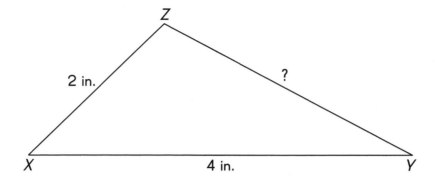

In triangle *XYZ*, the length of $\overline{ZY}$ is greater than 2 inches. A possible

length of $\overline{ZY}$, rounded to the nearest inch, is _____.

16.

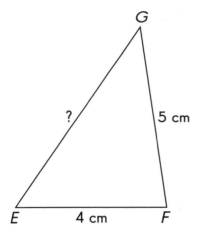

In triangle *EFG*, the length of $\overline{EG}$ is greater than 4 centimeters.

A possible length of $\overline{EG}$, rounded to the nearest centimeter, is

_____.

The lengths of two sides of each triangle are given. Name a possible length for the third side. The given lengths are in whole centimeters or whole inches.

17.

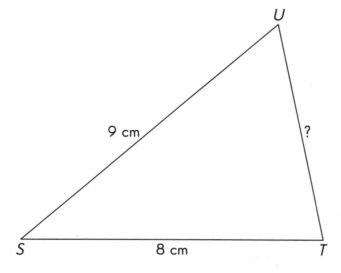

In triangle *STU*, the length of $\overline{UT}$ is less than 10 centimeters. A possible

length of $\overline{UT}$, rounded to the nearest centimeter, is _____.

18.

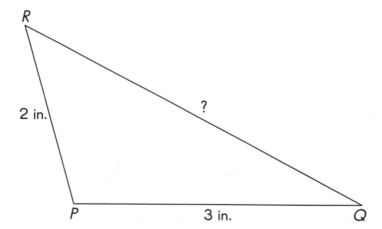

In triangle *PQR*, the length of $\overline{RQ}$ is greater than 3 inches. The possible

length of $\overline{RQ}$, rounded to the nearest inch, is _____.

Lesson 13.5   Parallelogram, Rhombus, and Trapezoid

Find the unknown angle measures. The figures are not drawn to scale.

1.   *DEFG* is a parallelogram and *GF* = *GH*.
Find the measure of ∠*y*.

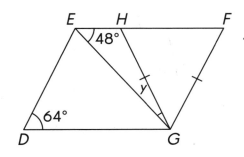

2.   *PQRS* is a parallelogram and *RST* is a right triangle.
Find the measures of ∠*PSR* and ∠*RST*.

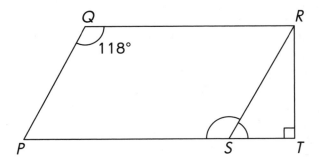

3.   *ABCD* and *ADEF* are parallelograms.
Find the measure of ∠*EDC*.

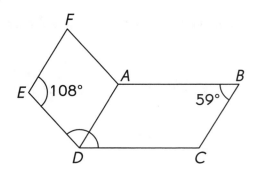

4.   *PQRS* is a rhombus and *PR* = *TR*.
Find the measure of ∠*PQR*.

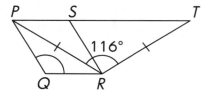

5. *WXYZ* is a rhombus and $\overline{WV}$ is a line segment.
Find the measure of $\angle VYZ$.

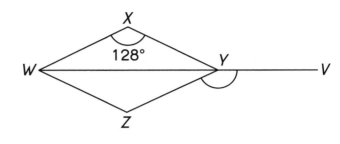

6. *ABCD* is a rhombus. $\overline{AE}$ is a line segment.
Find the measure of $\angle x$.

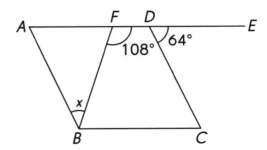

7.   PQRS is trapezoid and $\overline{SR} \parallel \overline{PQ}$.
SR = PR. Find the measure of $\angle PRQ$.

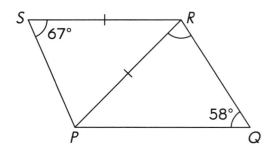

8.   ABCD is a trapezoid. $\overline{AB} \parallel \overline{DC}$ and CB = CD.
$\overleftrightarrow{FE}$ is a line.
Find the measure of $\angle BAD$.

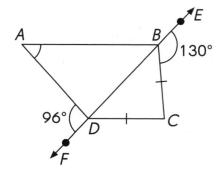

 **Put on Your Thinking Cap!**

The figures are not drawn to scale. Find the unknown angle measures.

1.   *PQRS* and *STUV* are parallelograms and *PT* = *PU*.
Find the measure of ∠*RSV*.

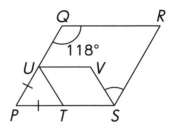

2.   *PQRS* is a parallelogram and *ST* = *SP*.
Find the measure of ∠*a*.

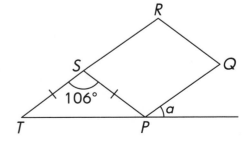

3. $ABCD$ is a square and $AEDF$ is a rhombus.
    Find the measure of $\angle CDE$.

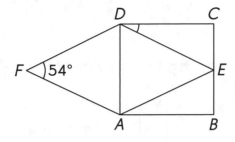

4. $BDEG$ is a trapezoid and $\overline{GF} \parallel \overline{BC}$.
    ABC and AEF are isosceles triangles.
    Find the measures of $\angle x$ and $\angle y$.

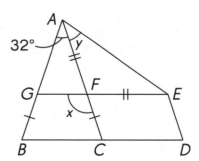

5.   In the figure, $PS = PR = RQ$ and the measure of $\angle STP$ is twice the measure of $\angle TPS$. Find the measures of $\angle x$ and $\angle y$.

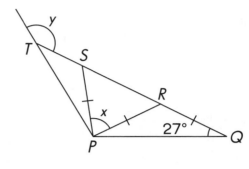

6. ABC is an equilateral triangle. CEF is an isosceles triangle, where $FC = FE$, m$\angle CED = 54°$, and m$\angle CFE = 118°$.
Find the measures of $\angle x$ and $\angle y$.

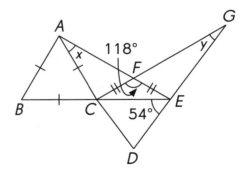

7. *ABCD* is a rectangle. *FA = FE* and *FB = FG*.
Find the measures of ∠*x* and ∠*y*.

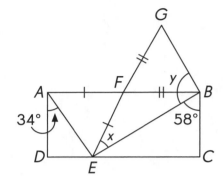

8. *ABC* is a right triangle, $\overline{BG}$ is a line segment, and m∠*ABC* = m∠*CDE*.
m∠*ACB* = 90° and $\overline{AB} \parallel \overline{DE}$. Find the measures of ∠*x* and ∠*y*.

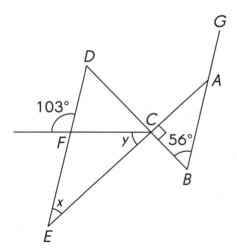

CHAPTER 14 · Three-Dimensional Shapes

Lesson 14.1   Prisms and Pyramids

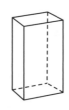
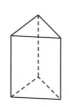

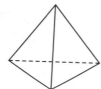

The flat surface of a solid is called a face.
Two faces meet at an edge.
Edges meet at a vertex.
The mathematical name for corners is vertices.

Complete the table.

	Solid	Number of Faces (F)	Number of Vertices (V)	Number of Edges (E)
1.	cube			
2.	rectangular prism			
3.	triangular prism			
4.	square pyramid			
5.	triangular pyramid			

Complete.

6. What general statement can you make about the number of faces, the number of vertices, and the number of edges of prisms and pyramids?

    _____

    _____

    _____

    _____

7. Which of these nets can be folded to form a cube?
    Shade the circles that represent the correct answers.

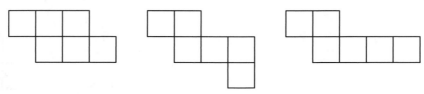

○   ○   ○

○   ○   ○

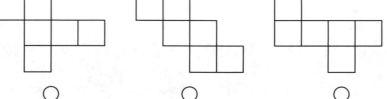

○   ○   ○

8. Which of these nets can be folded to form a rectangular prism?
Shade the circles that represent the correct answers.

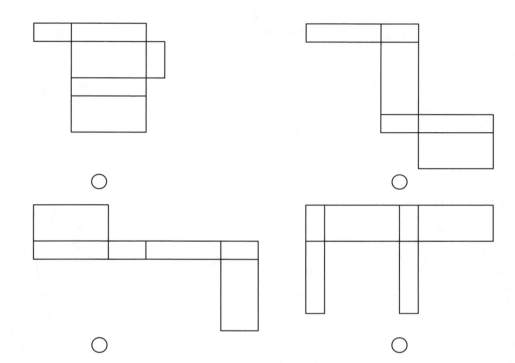

9. Which of these nets can be folded to form a triangular prism?
Shade the circles that represent the correct answers.

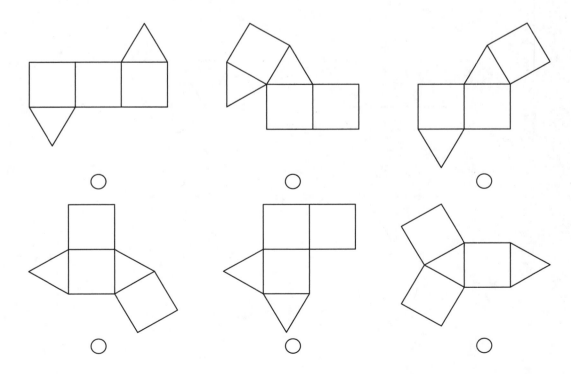

10.   Which of these nets can be folded to form a square pyramid?
Shade the circles that represent the correct answers.

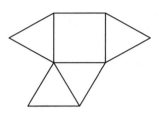

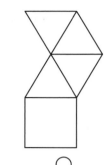

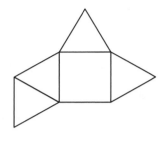

○

○

○

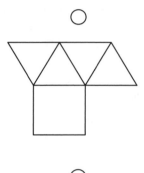

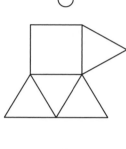

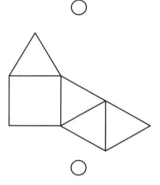

○

○

○

11.   Which of the nets can be folded to form a triangular pyramid? Shade the
circles that represent the correct answers.

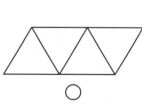

○

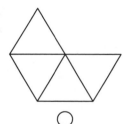

○

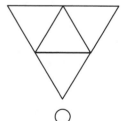

○

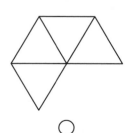

○

Lesson 14.2   Cylinder, Sphere, and Cone

Complete.

1.

A cylinder has _____ congruent circular faces and _____ curved surface.

Which of these nets can be folded to form a cylinder? Shade the circle that represents the correct answer.

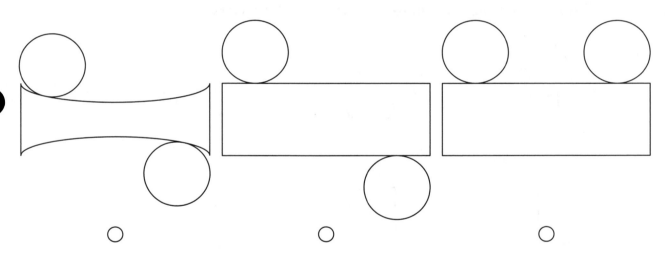

2.

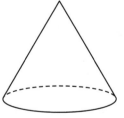

A cone has _____ curved surface.

Which of these nets can be folded to form a cone? Shade the circle that represents the correct answer.

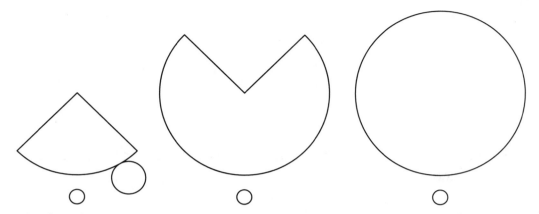

3. Which of these three-dimensional figures have no vertices? Shade the circles that represent the correct answers.

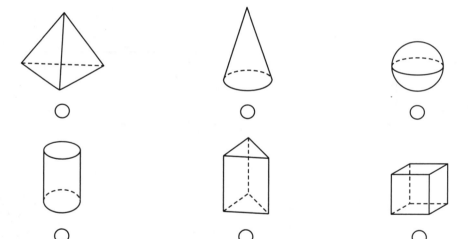

Write _T_ for _True_ and _F_ for _False_.

4. A pyramid has a curved surface.   (   )

5. A prism has two parallel bases.   (   )

6. A cone has three vertices.   (   )

7. A cube has triangular faces.   (   )

8. A cylinder has two parallel bases.   (   )

9. A sphere has a curved surface.   (   )

 Put on Your Thinking Cap!

Determine the number of faces, edges, and vertices each figure has.

  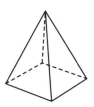

 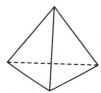

The flat surface of a solid is called a face.
The line segment where two faces meet is an edge.
Edges meet at a vertex.

Complete the table.

	Solid	Number of Faces (F)	Number of Edges (E)	Number of Vertices (V)	F + V − E
1.	cube				
2.	cone				
3.	triangular prism				
4.	square pyramid				
5.	triangular pyramid				
6.	cylinder				

Name: _____ Date: _____

Identical sticks were used to form a series of vertical three-dimensional structures. The first three shapes are shown below.

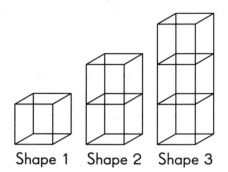

Shape 1   Shape 2   Shape 3

Complete the table.

7.

Shape	Number of Cubes	Number of Sticks Used	Total Surface Area (length of each stick is 1 unit)
1	1	12	6
2	2	20	10
3	3	28	14
4	4	?	?
5	5	?	?

Solve. Show your work.

8.   How many sticks are needed to form Shape 10?

CHAPTER 15

Surface Area and Volume

Lesson 15.1   Building Solids Using Unit Cubes

How many unit cubes are used to build each solid?

1.

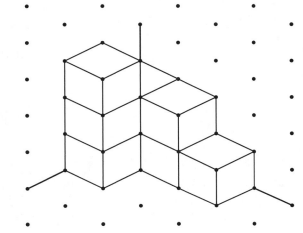

_____ unit cubes

2.

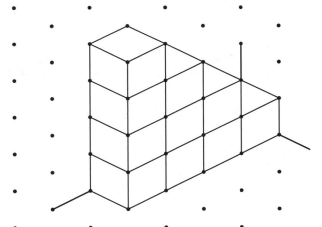

_____ unit cubes

3.

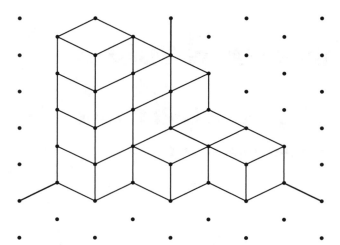

_____ unit cubes

4.

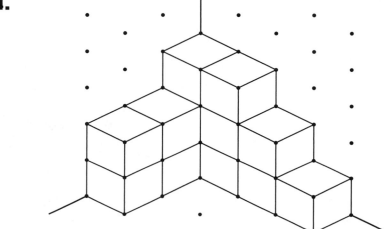

_____ unit cubes

5.

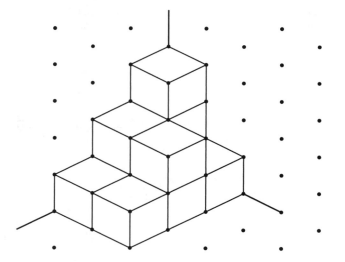

_____ unit cubes

© 2009 Marshall Cavendish International (Singapore) Private Limited. Copying is permitted; see page ii.

Lesson 15.2   Drawing Cubes and Rectangular Prisms
Draw on dot paper.

1.   Draw a unit cube.

2.   Draw two different views of a rectangular prism made up of 2 unit cubes.

3.   Draw a cube made up of 8 unit cubes.

Draw these cubes or rectangular prisms on the dot paper.

4.

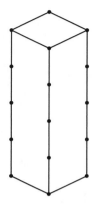

5.

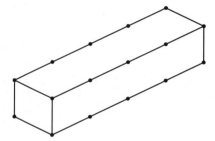

6.

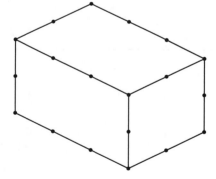

7.

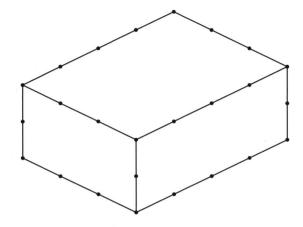

8.

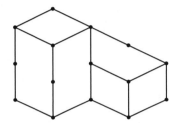

9.

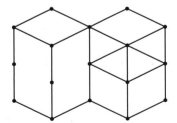

10.

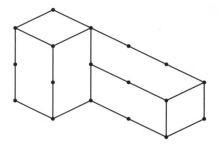

11.

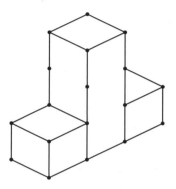

12.

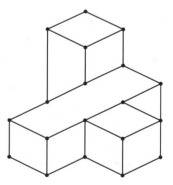

Complete the drawing of each cube or rectangular prism.

13.

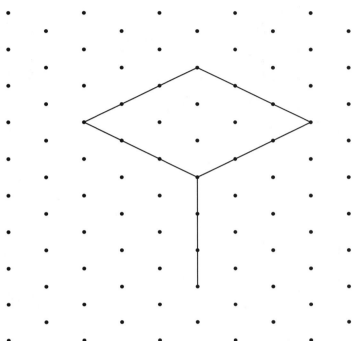

14.

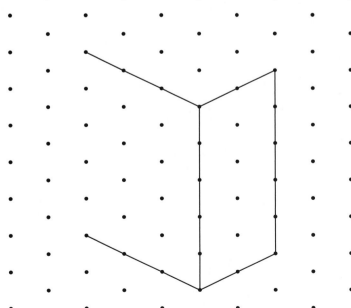

15.

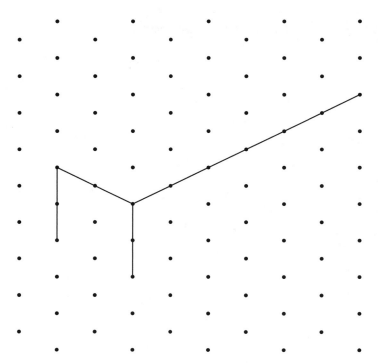

16.

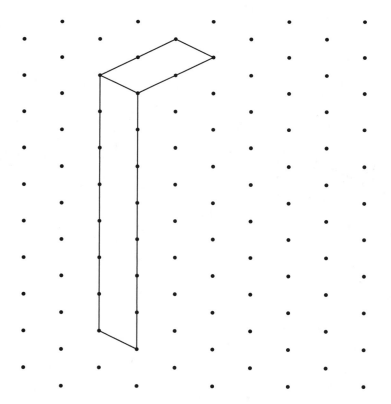

Lesson 15.3   Nets and Surface Area

Find the surface area.

1.   The diagram shows the net of a cube.
Find the surface area of the cube.

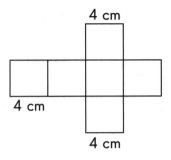

4 cm

4 cm

4 cm

2.   The diagram shows the net of a rectangular prism.
Find the surface area of the rectangular prism.

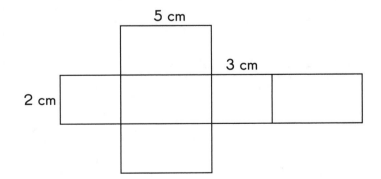

5 cm

3 cm

2 cm

The diagrams show the nets of cubes or rectangular prisms.
Find the surface area of each cube or rectangular prism.

3.

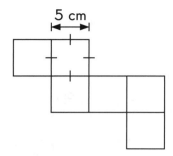

4.

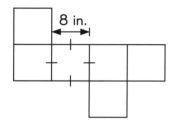

5.

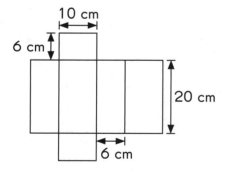

6.

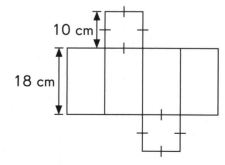

Name: _____   **Date:** _____

Find the surface area of each cube or rectangular prism.

7.

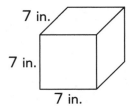

7 in.

7 in.

7 in.

8.

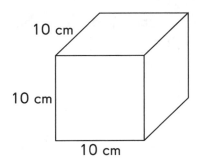

10 cm

10 cm

10 cm

9.

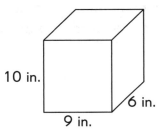

10 in.

6 in.

9 in.

10.

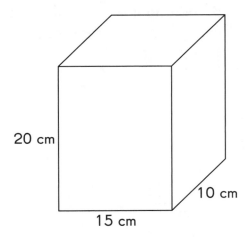

20 cm

10 cm

15 cm

11.

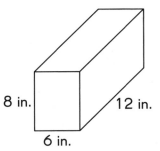

8 in.

12 in.

6 in.

12.

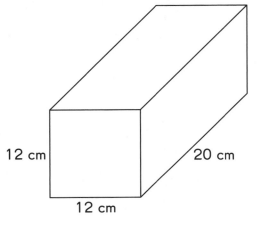

12 cm

20 cm

12 cm

Solve. Show your work.

13. The surface area of a cube is 216 square centimeters. Find the length of the cube.

14. A rectangular piece of wood has a length of 30 centimeters and a square base with sides that measure 6 centimeters. What is the surface area of the piece of wood?

15. An open rectangular water tank measures 20 inches by 18 inches by 16 inches. The tank is full of water. Find the total surface area of the tank that is in contact with the water.

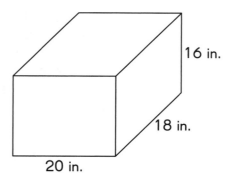

16 in.

18 in.

20 in.

Lesson 15.4   Understanding and Measuring Volume

These solids are formed by stacking unit cubes in the corner of a room. Find the volume of each solid.

1.

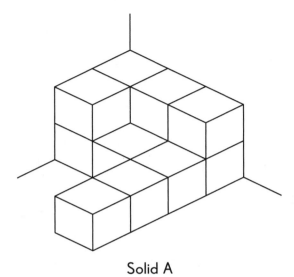

Solid A

Volume = _____ cubic units

2.

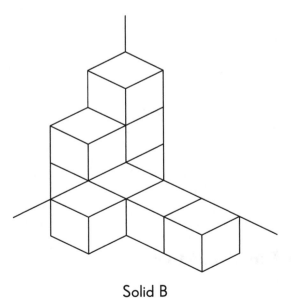

Solid B

Volume = _____ cubic units

3.

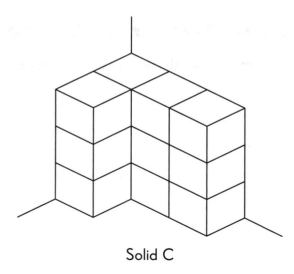

Solid C

Volume = _____ cubic units

4.

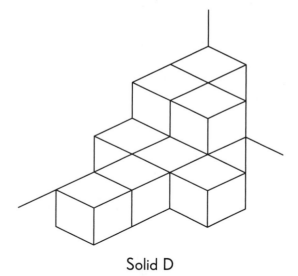

Solid D

Volume = _____ cubic units

Compare the volumes of the solids in Exercises 1 to 4. Then fill in the blanks.

5. Solid _____ has the smallest volume.

6. Solid _____ and Solid _____ have the same volume.

Name: _____ **Date:** _____

These solids are formed by stacking unit cubes in the corner of a room. Find the volume of each solid.

7.

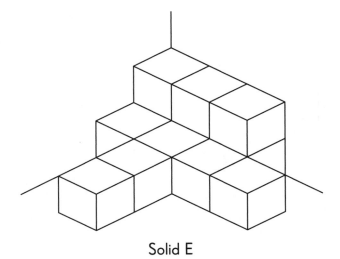

Solid E

Volume = _____ cm³

8.

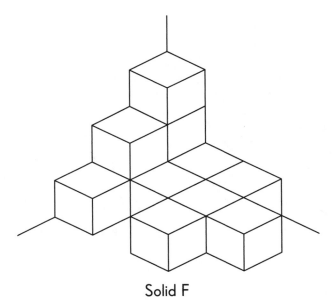

Solid F

Volume = _____ cm³

9.

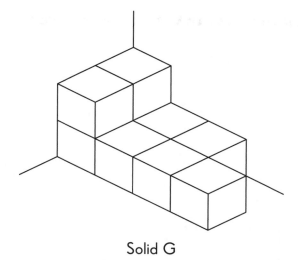

Solid G

Volume = _____ cm^3

10.

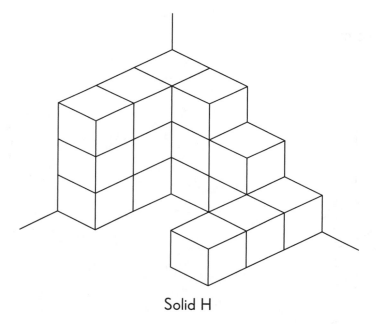

Solid H

Volume = _____ cm^3

**Compare the volumes of the solids in Exercises 7 to 10.
Then fill in the blanks.**

11. Solid _____ has the smallest volume.

12. Solid _____ has the largest volume.

13. Solid _____ and Solid _____ have the same volume.

**These solids are built using 1-centimeter cubes.
Find the volume of each solid. Then fill in the blanks.**

14.

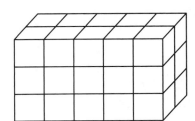

15.

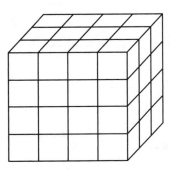

Length = _____ cm

Width = _____ cm

Height = _____ cm

Volume = _____ cm³

Length = _____ cm

Width = _____ cm

Height = _____ cm

Volume = _____ cm³

16.

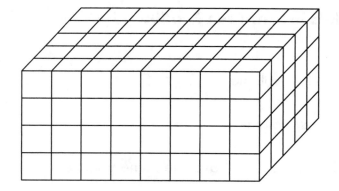

Length = _____ cm

Width = _____ cm

Height = _____ cm

Volume = _____ cm³

17.

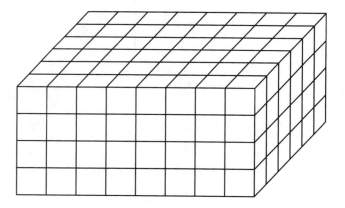

Length = _____ cm

Width = _____ cm

Height = _____ cm

Volume = _____ cm³

Lesson 15.5   Volume of a Rectangular Prism and Liquid

Find the volume of each rectangular prism.

1.

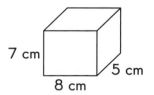

Length = _____ cm

Width = _____ cm

Height = _____ cm

Volume = _____ × _____ × _____

= _____ cm^3

2.

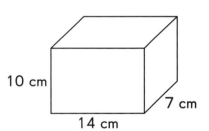

Length = _____ cm

Width = _____ cm

Height = _____ cm

Volume = _____ × _____ × _____

= _____ cm^3

Find the volume of each rectangular prism.

3.

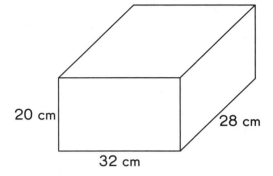

20 cm

28 cm

32 cm

Length = _____ cm

Width = _____ cm

Height = _____ cm

Volume = _____ $\times$ _____ $\times$ _____

= _____ cm^3

4.

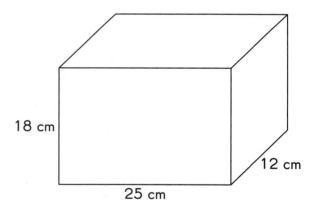

18 cm

12 cm

25 cm

Volume = _____ $\times$ _____ $\times$ _____

= _____ cm^3

5.

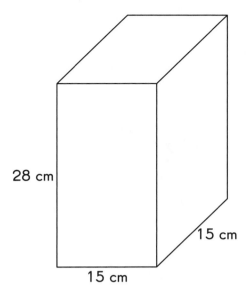

28 cm

15 cm

15 cm

Volume = _____ × _____ × _____

= _____ cm³

Find the length of the unknown edge of each rectangular prism.

6.

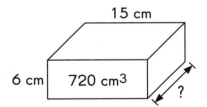

15 cm

6 cm   720 cm³   ?

Width = _____ cm

7.

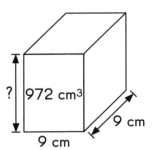

?   972 cm³   9 cm

9 cm

Height = _____ cm

8.

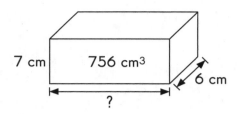

7 cm | 756 cm³
6 cm
?

Length = _____ cm

9. The figure is a rectangular prism with a square base.

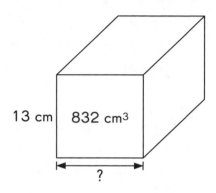

13 cm | 832 cm³
?

Length = _____ cm

Write each measure in cubic centimeters.

10. 390 mL = _____ cm³   **11.** 1 L 125 mL = _____ cm³

12. 2 L 600 mL = _____ cm³   **13.** 4 L 80 mL = _____ cm³

14. 5 L 50 mL = _____ cm³   **15.** 2 L 6 mL = _____ cm³

Write each measure in liters and milliliters or liters.

16. 890 cm³ = _____ L _____ mL

17. 1,850 cm³ = _____ L _____ mL

18. 3,065 cm³ = _____ L _____ mL

19. 530 cm³ = _____ L   **20.** 755 cm³ = _____ L

21. 1,650 cm³ = _____ L   **22.** 2,075 cm³ = _____ L

Find the volume of water in each rectangular tank in milliliters.
Hint: 1 cm³ = 1 mL

23.

15 cm

16 cm

26 cm

Volume = _____

24.

12 cm

18 cm

32 cm

Volume = _____

Find the volume of water in each rectangular tank in liters.
Hint: 1 cm³ = 1 mL
**   1,000 cm³ = 1 L**

25.

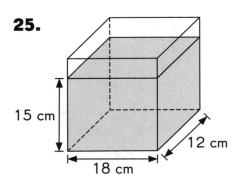

15 cm

12 cm

18 cm

Volume = _____

26.

28 cm

15 cm

20 cm

Volume = _____

Solve. Show your work.

27. A rectangular fish tank measures 38 centimeters by 23 centimeters by 18 centimeters. How much water is in the tank when it is $\frac{2}{3}$-full? Give your answer in liters and milliliters.

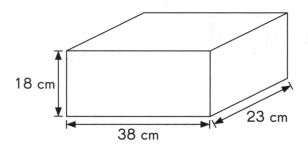

28. A rectangular tank measuring 30 centimeters long, 22 centimeters wide, and 25 centimeters high is $\frac{4}{5}$-full of water. If $\frac{1}{4}$ of the water is removed, what is the volume of water left in the tank? Give your answer in liters.

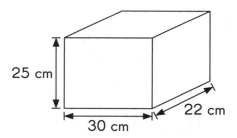

29. A rectangular tank measuring 42 centimeters by 20 centimeters by 24 centimeters is filled with water to a height of 7 centimeters. What is the volume of water needed to fill the tank completely? Give your answer in liters.

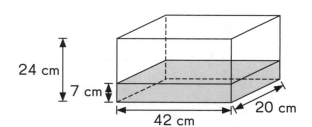

© 2009 Marshall Cavendish International (Singapore) Private Limited. Copying is permitted; see page ii.

Put on Your Thinking Cap!

Solve. Show your work.

1. Jessica used 35 unit cubes to build the solid shown. Another row of cubes is to be placed below the bottom row following the same pattern. How many more cubes will Jessica need?

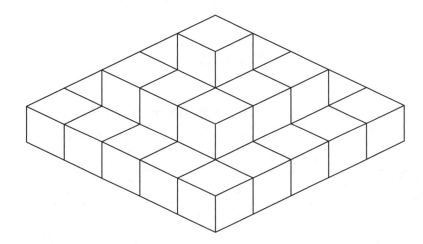

2. Paul uses 5 unit cubes to build the first figure and 8 unit cubes to build the second figure into the T-shaped patterns shown.

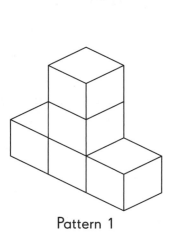

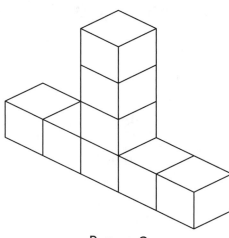

Pattern 1   Pattern 2

a. Paul continues to build the third and fourth patterns. Find the number of unit cubes in Patterns 3 and 4. Record your answers in the table.

T-Shaped Pattern	1	2	3	4
Number of Unit Cubes	5	$5 + 3 = 8$		

b. How many cubes would be used to build Patterns 5 and 6?

c. Find the number of unit cubes in Pattern 10.

3. The solid is made up of identical cubes glued together. The surface area of the solid is painted blue. The volume of the solid is 960 cubic centimeters. Find the surface area that is painted blue.

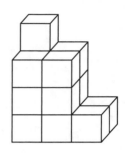

4. In order to fill the box completely, 126 3-centimeter cubes are needed. What is the height of the box?

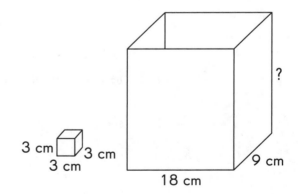

5.   The solid is made up of 3-centimeter cubes.

   a.   Find the volume of the solid.

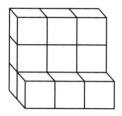

   b.   Find the surface area of the solid.

   c.   The whole solid is painted red.

   i.   Find the number of cubes that have only two faces painted red.

   ii.   Find the number of cubes that have only three faces painted red.

   iii.   Find the number of cubes that have only four faces painted red.

6. Two wooden blocks, A and B, are glued together. The ratio of the volume of block A to the volume of block B is 3 : 7.

a. What is the volume of block B?

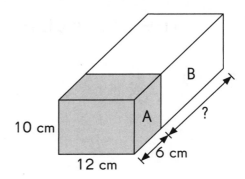

10 cm

12 cm

6 cm

?

A

B

b. What is the width of block B?

7. A cubic container was completely filled with water. When $\frac{3}{4}$ of the water from the container was poured into a rectangular tank, the tank became $\frac{1}{4}$ full. The capacity of the tank is 1.024 liters more than that of the cubic container. Find the length of the cubic container.

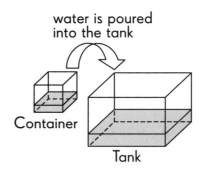

water is poured into the tank

Container

Tank

8. John wanted to build a model wall measuring 36 centimeters long, 8 centimeters wide, and 21 centimeters high. He used blocks that measured 3 centimeters by 4 centimeters by 2 centimeters. John stopped after building $\frac{5}{9}$ of the wall. How many more blocks will John need to complete the wall?

9. How many 2-centimeter cubes can be packed into a rectangular prism measuring 25 centimeters by 15 centimeters by 20 centimeters?

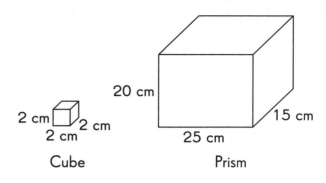

Cube   Prism

10. Identical watch boxes each measuring 10 centimeters by 8 centimeters by 6 centimeters are packed in a rectangular container measuring 54 centimeters by 44 centimeters by 22 centimeters. What is the maximum number of watch boxes that can be packed into the container?

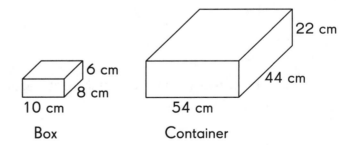

Box   Container

11.   Two identical rectangular cards measuring 20 centimeters by 12 centimeters are folded to form two different rectangular solids.

    a.   One of the solids is shown below. Label its width and height.

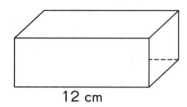

                                                           12 cm

    b.   Draw the other rectangular solid. Label its length, width, and height.

    c.   Find the volume of each rectangular solid.

End-of-Year Test

⌗ **100**

Multiple Choice (20 × 2 points = 40 points)

Fill in the circle next to the correct answer.

1. Estimate the result of 88,950 ÷ 295.

(A) 100   (B) 200   (C) 300   (D) 400

2. Complete the pattern.

185, 190, 200, 215, 235, _____

(A) 250   (B) 255   (C) 260   (D) 265

3. What is the value of $3 \times 18 - 8 \div 2$?

(A) 15   (B) 23   (C) 50   (D) 58

4. What is the difference in value between the digit 6 and the digit 4 in the number 765,420?

(A) 2   (B) 200   (C) 59,600   (D) 64,580

5. Jenny buys 1,790 packets of snacks. She packs 50 packets in each container. How many containers does Jenny need?

(A) 35   (B) 36   (C) 37   (D) 38

6. Jane and Chantrelle had an equal number of crackers. After Chantrelle ate some of her crackers, the ratio of the number of Jane's crackers to the number of Chantrelle's crackers was 7 : 3. If Chantrelle had 36 crackers less than Jane, how many crackers did Jane have?

(A) 27   (B) 28   (C) 48   (D) 63

7. *ABCD* is a square with a side length of 16 centimeters.
AE = *ED* = *DF.* Find the area of the shaded part.

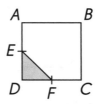

(A) 16 cm²   (B) 32 cm²   (C) 64 cm²   (D) 128 cm²

8. The ratio of the amount of water in Container A to the amount af water in Container B is 5 : 6 at first. Then, $\frac{3}{5}$ of the water in Container A is poured into Container B. After that, $\frac{2}{3}$ of the water in Container B is poured into Container A. What is the new ratio of the amount of water in Container A to the amout of water in Container B?

(A) 8 : 3   (B) 3 : 8   (C) 6 : 5   (D) 4 : 7

9. A number is twice a smaller number. The average of the two numbers is 117. What is the larger number?

(A) 78   (B) 156   (C) 176   (D) 234

Name: _____   **Date:** _____

10. In the diagram, *ABCD* is a rectangle. *AE* = *EF* = *FG* = *GB*. What fraction of the figure is unshaded?

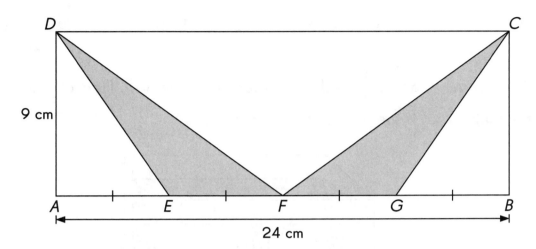

(A) $\frac{1}{4}$ (B) $\frac{1}{2}$ (C) $\frac{3}{4}$ (D) $\frac{3}{5}$

11. On the playground, 10 children line up in a row. They are of equal distances apart. The first child is 23 meters 40 centimeters away from the last child. How far apart are the first child and the fourth child?

(A) 7 m 20 cm   (B) 7 m 80 cm

(C) 9 m 36 cm   (D) 10 m 40 cm

12. $\frac{1}{4}$ of the average of two numbers is 90. One of the numbers is 200.

What is the other number?

(A) 120   (B) 160   (C) 260   (D) 520

13. Carol and Ruth had a total of $34.70. After their mother gave $9.05 to Carol, she had 4 times as much money as Ruth. How much money did Carol have at first?

(A) $8.75   (B) $25.95   (C) $29.57   (D) $435.00

14. A jug is 80% full of water. After 360 milliliters of water are poured out, the jug is 60%-filled with water. What is the capacity of the jug?

(A) 1.8 L   (B) 1.44 L   (C) 1.08 L   (D) 0.72 L

15. A rectangular tank is $\frac{3}{4}$-filled with water. There are 14.4 liters of water in the tank. What is the height of the tank?

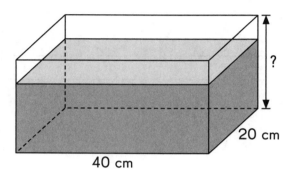

20 cm

40 cm

(A) 16 cm   (B) 20 cm   (C) 24 cm   (D) 28 cm

16. Of the 600 stamps in an album, 52% are local stamps and the rest are foreign stamps. How many more local stamps than foreign stamps are there in the album?

(A) 24   (B) 240   (C) 288   (D) 312

17. The ratio of Adam's books to Brandon's books is 5 : 4. The ratio of Brandon's books to Colin's books is 3 : 2. Colin has 56 books. How many books does Adam have?

(A) 28   (B) 84   (C) 105   (D) 140

18. Shaun bought 4 different rackets. The first racket cost $49.50 and the average cost of the remaining rackets was $\frac{2}{3}$ the cost of the first racket. How much did Shaun pay for the rackets?

(A) $82.50   (B) $99   (C) $123.75   (D) $148.50

19. Kaylee has 76 more beads than Alicia, and $\frac{3}{5}$ of Alicia's beads is equal to $\frac{1}{3}$ of Kaylee's beads. How many beads does Kaylee have?

(A) 266   (B) 171   (C) 95   (D) 19

20. There are 550 stickers in a sticker book. 20% of the stickers belong to Jane and 40% belong to Sam. Find the difference in the number of stickers that each child has.

(A) 330   (B) 110   (C) 220   (D) 44

Short Answer (20 × 2 points = 40 points)

Write your answer in the space given.

21. When the spinner is spun, what is the theoretical probability that the pointer will stop on numbers which are factors of 6?

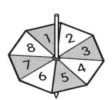

Answer: _____

22. What is the value of 58,200 ÷ 3,000?

Answer: _____

23. Evaluate $4\frac{1}{3} - 1\frac{3}{5} + 3\frac{1}{2}$.

Answer: _____

24. Simplify $10d - 3d + 8 - 5d - 2$.

Answer: _____

25. Gary has $5y$ comic books. Shaun has $2y$ more comic books than Gary. Susan has 6 less comic books than Shaun. How many comic books do they have in all?

Answer: _____ comic books

26. Leona has 5 dolls and 10 doll dresses. Find the number of combinations of dressing up the dolls.

Answer: _____ combinations

27. Chester has $\frac{7}{8}$ kilogram of beef. He uses $\frac{2}{5}$ of it to make a stew. How much beef does Chester have left?

Answer: _____ kilogram of beef

28. Jane has 84 beads. She gives $\frac{3}{4}$ of them to Jack. Jack gives $\frac{2}{7}$ of what he receives to Karen. How many beads does Karen get?

Answer: _____ beads

29. In the election for class president, there were two candidates, Joel and Sean. Joel got 60% of the votes, which was 38 votes more than Sean. Find the total number of votes cast.

Answer: _____ votes

30. Photo B is an enlargement of Photo A. Photo A measures 4 centimeters by 3 centimeters. What is the area of Photo B?

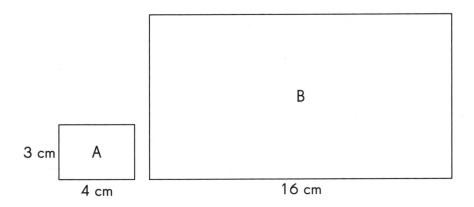

3 cm   A

4 cm

B

16 cm

Answer: _____ cm²

31.   Find the area of the shaded region in the figure.

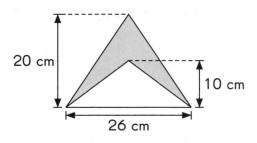

Answer: _____ cm²

32.   Find the surface area of the rectangular prism.

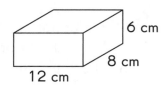

Answer: _____ cm²

33.   The rectangular prism is made up of identical cubes. The volume of the rectangular prism is 1,620 cubic centimeters. Find the length of each cube.

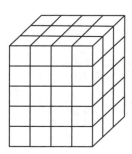

Answer: _____ cm

Name: _____   Date: _____

34. Find the volume of water in the rectangular tank.
Hint: 1 L = 1,000 cm³

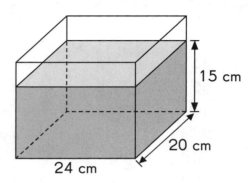

15 cm

20 cm

24 cm

Answer: _____ L

35. A gas tank contains 3 liters of gas. The graph shows the rate at which gas is pumped into the tank during the next 8 seconds. Use the graph to find the volume of gas added to the tank in 6 seconds.
Hint: Gas is pumped into the tank at a rate of 1 liter every 2 seconds.

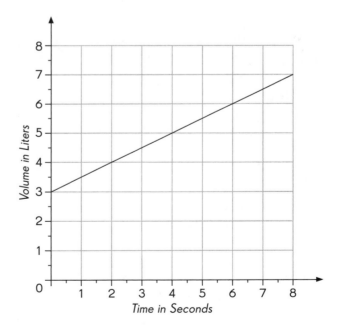

Answer: _____ L

A company owns five shops. The graph shows the number of computers sold in September and October.
Study the graph and answer Exercises 36 and 37.

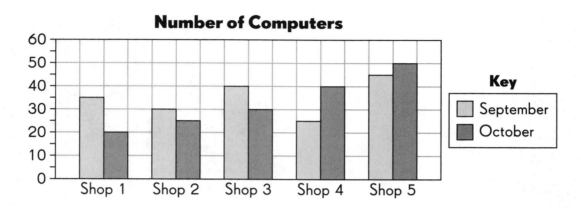

Number of Computers

Key
☐ September
■ October

36.   Find the total number of computers sold in the five shops in September.

Answer: _____ computers

37.   Which shop had the greatest increase in the number of computers sold from September to October? What was the increase?

Answer: Shop _____

_____

38. In the figure, *ABC* is an equilateral triangle and *BC* = *CD*. Find the measure of ∠*ACD*.

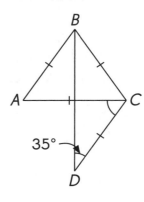

Answer: m∠*ACD* _____

39. *PQR* is an isosceles triangle and *QP* = *QR*. $\overline{PT}$ is a line segment. Find the measure of ∠*RQT*.

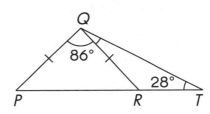

Answer: m∠*RQT* _____

40. *ABCD* is a parallelogram. *ED* = *EF*. Find the measure of ∠*AEF*.

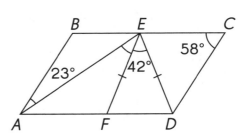

Answer: m∠*AEF* _____

Extended Response (5 × 4 points = 20 points)

Solve. Show your work.

41. Lincoln spends $95 of his pocket money every month and saves the rest. This month he decides to spend only $75, thereby increasing his savings by 40%. How much pocket money does Lincoln have every month?

42. The figure is not drawn to scale. The figure is a rectangle that is divided into 6 parts. Each part has a different area. The side lengths are whole numbers.

a. Find the total area of P and Q.

40 cm²	P	32 cm²
25 cm²	30 cm²	Q

b. Find the perimeter of the figure.

43. Alex, Benny, and Cindy shared a bag of marbles in the ratio 3 : 5 : 2. During a game, Alex lost half of his marbles to Benny. Benny lost 18 marbles to Cindy. Cindy had twice as many marbles as Alex at the end of the game.

   a. How many marbles did Alex have before the game?

   b. How many marbles did Benny have at the end of the game?

44. Roy had 6 times as many stamps as Cynthia. After their friend gave 4 stamps to Roy and 16 stamps to Cynthia, Roy had 4 times as many stamps as Cynthia. How many stamps did Roy have in the end?

45. At a school's athletic meet, $\frac{2}{7}$ of the number of spectators was equal to $\frac{3}{5}$ of the number of participants.

a. What fraction of the number of spectators was the number of participants?

b. There were 253 more spectators than participants. How many spectators were at the athletic meet?

Answers

Chapter 8

Lesson 8.1

1. 2.045

2. 6.308

3. 0.175

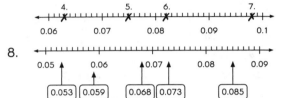

8.

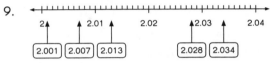

9.

10. 60
11. 212
12. 58
13. 3
14. 2
15. 0; 4
16. 0.009
17. 0.025
18. 0.416
19. 1.055
20. 0.005
21. 0.078
22. 0.110 or 0.11
23. 0.603
24. 2.508
25. 2.640 or 2.64
26. 3.009
27. 4.567
28. 1.004
29. 3.082
30. 5.606
31. 7.190 or 7.19
32. 217
33. 6
34. 95
35. 1,702

36. $8 + \frac{7}{10} + \frac{6}{100} + \frac{4}{1000}$

37. $3 + \frac{5}{10} + \frac{2}{100} + \frac{3}{1000}$

38. 5 + 0.2 + 0.01 + 0.003

39. 1 + 0.9 + 0.04 + 0.005

40. thousandths

41. 0

42. tenths

43. 9 ones

Lesson 8.2

1. 5.078 is greater than 4.087; 5.078 > 4.087

2. 0.654 is less than 0.945; 0.654 < 0.945

3. 4.720 is greater than 4.270; 4.720 > 4.270

4. <   5. >

6. <   7. >

8. greatest: 5.69; least: 5.069

9. greatest: 80.202; least: 80.002

10. 0.569, 0.956, 0.965

11. 6.309, 6.903, 9.036

12. 0.088, 0.8, 0.808, 0.88

13. 0.029, 0.1, 0.999, 1

14. 4.33; 4.32

15. 7.00 or 7; 7.01

16. 3.46

17. 12.015; 12.02

18. 2.295; 2.30

19.

Decimal	Rounded to the Nearest		
	Whole Number	Tenth	Hundredth
2.768	3	2.8	2.77
3.184	3	3.2	3.18
0.476	0	0.5	0.48
8.695	9	8.7	8.70

20. Any answer from 1.45 to 1.54.

21. Any answer from 4.255 to 4.264.

22. Any answer from 8.031 to 8.034.

23. Any answer from 7.905 to 7.909.

Lesson 8.3

1. $\frac{16}{25}$ 2. $1\frac{11}{50}$ 3. $2\frac{29}{50}$ 4. $3\frac{9}{100}$

5. $\frac{9}{250}$ 6. $\frac{111}{1000}$ 7. $1\frac{9}{100}$ 8. $2\frac{73}{200}$

9. $2\frac{16}{25}$ 10. $5\frac{3}{4}$ 11. $7\frac{1}{125}$ 12. $10\frac{357}{1000}$

Put on Your Thinking Cap!

Thinking skill: Classifying

1. 58   2. 209   3. 402

4. 2,067   5. 3,504   6. 953

Thinking skill: Classifying

7. 17   8. 17.0   9. 17.00

Thinking skill: Identifying patterns and relationships

Strategy: Look for a pattern

10. 9.78

11. 5.00 or 5

12. 16.8

13. 15.5

14. 21.6

Chapter 9

Lesson 9.1

1. 9; 36; 3.6
2. 15; 45; 4.5
3. 8; 40; 0.40
4. 27; 162; 1.62
5. 36; 252; 2.52
6. 4.8
7. 24.5
8. 35.1
9. 26.1
10. 27.6
11. 37.0
12. 73.6
13. 0.42
14. 0.63
15. 42.88
16. 28.16
17. 22.90
18. 33.84
19. 75.24

Lesson 9.2

1. 48.5
2. 3.75
3. 492.8
4. 230
5. 10
6. 66.22
7. 100
8. 4.03
9. 1,000
10. 0.108
11. 10; 100; 1,000
12. 401.6; 40.16; 4.016
13. 6; 5.724; 57.24
14. 8; 3.008; 300.8
15. 3; 2.91; 2,910
16. 25
17. 112
18. 4,770
19. 43,716
20. 0.085 kg × 200 + 0.56 kg = 17.56 kg
    The total mass of the box and
    200 paperweights is 17.56 kilograms.

Lesson 9.3

1. 8; 4; 0.4
2. 24; 6; 0.6
3. 9; 3; 0.03
4. 63; 9; 0.09
5. 153; 17; 0.17
6. 2.3
7. 3.7
8. 3.2
9. 0.06
10. 11.33
11. 5.88
12. 0.8
13. 0.7
14. 2.59
15. 2.08

Lesson 9.4

1. 0.236
2. 3.015
3. 5.082
4. 2.1
5. 0.78
6. 82.3
7. 10
8. 345
9. 100
10. 6,920
11. 1,000
12. 48,000
13. 10; 1,990; 19,900
14. 82.35; 100; 1,000
15. 40.1; 401; 4,010
16. 10; 100; 1,000
17. 2; 149; 14.9
18. 8; 4; 0.04
19. 6; 200; 0.2
20. 7.5
21. 0.81
22. 0.092
23. 0.64
24. 0.35
25. 2.08
26. 125 L ÷ 500 = 0.25 L
    0.25 liter of apple juice is in each cup.
27. 370 m ÷ 2,000 = 0.185 m
    The length of each cut piece of string is
    0.185 meter.
28. Cost of 1 file = $97.50 ÷ 30
    = $3.25
    Cost of 1 book = $3.25 × 10
    = $32.50
    The cost of each book is $32.50.
29. Cost of 10 pears and 10 oranges
    = $0.94 × 10 = $9.40
    Cost of 1 orange = $10.05 − $9.40
    = $0.65
    The cost of 1 orange was $0.65.

Lesson 9.5

1. $16
2. $70
3. $80
4. $70
5. 50
6. 320
7. 270
8. 7
9. 11
10. 24
11. 23.1 km
12. 4.3 kg
13. 68.4 kg
14. 1.2 L
15. $4.95 × 4 ≈ $5 × 4 = $20
    The cost of 4 tins is about $20.
16. 175 cm ÷ 18.5 cm ≈ 180 cm ÷ 20 cm = 9
    Vivien uses her handspan 9 times to measure
    the length.

Lesson 9.6

1. 1.25 L × 8 = 10 L
   There are 10 liters of orange juice in 8 bottles.

2.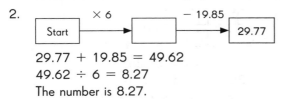

   29.77 + 19.85 = 49.62
   49.62 ÷ 6 = 8.27
   The number is 8.27.

3. 1.38 km × 2 = 2.76 km
   2.76 km × 3 = 8.28 km
   Brian rides his bike 8.28 kilometers in all.

4. a. 0.85 L × 9 = 7.65 L
   Teresa adds 7.65 liters of water.
   b. 7.65 L + 0.85 L = 8.5 L
   1 L of drinks ⟶ 4 cups
   8.5 L of drinks ⟶ 8.5 × 4 = 34 cups
   Teresa can make 34 cups of juice.

5. 4 pencils ⟶ $1.90
   14 pencils ⟶ $\frac{\$1.90}{4} \times 14 = \$6.65$
   The cost of 14 pencils is $6.65.

6. (5.81 − 3.8) ÷ 3 = 0.67
   3.8 − 0.67 × 5 = 0.45
   The mass of the empty container is 0.45 kilogram.

7. 100 g of ham ⟶ $1.50
   1,000 g (1 kg) ⟶ $1.50 × 10 = $15
   1.2 kg ⟶ $15 + $1.50 × 2 = $18
   1.2 kilograms of ham cost $18.
   100 g of sausages ⟶ $1.50 + $0.85
                      = $2.35
   600 g ⟶ $2.35 × 6 = $14.10
   600 grams of sausages cost $14.10.
   $18 + $14.10 = $32.10
   Paul pays $32.10.

8. 30.0 − (2.7 × 4) m = 19.2 m
                      = 1,920 cm
   1,920 ÷ 75 ≈ 25
   The maximum number of presents she could tie is 25.

9. 12 cakes ⟶ 10 × $1.50 = $15
   100 ÷ 12 = 8 R 4
   ($15 × 8) + ($1.50 × 4) = $126
   Maria will need to spend $126 in all.

10. $5,120 − (160 × $3.50) = $4,560
    $4,560 ÷ $(8.50 + 3.50) = 380 adults
    380 + 160 = 540
    540 children visited the exhibition.

11. ▭ + ◯◯◯ = 1,020 g
    ▭ + ◯◯◯ = 2,160 g
        ◯◯◯
        ◯◯◯

    6 balls ⟶ 2.16 kg − 1.02 kg = 1.14 kg
    3 balls ⟶ 1.14 kg ÷ 2 = 0.57 kg
    Empty box ⟶ 1.02 kg − 0.57 kg = 0.45 kg
    The mass of the empty box is 0.45 kilogram.

12. Paul's Stall ⟶ $2.20 × 10 = $22 per kg
    Sam's Stall ⟶ $11.00 × 2 = $22 per kg
    a. Paul's stall and Sam's stall sell shrimp for
       $22 per kilogram.
    b. $(22 − 19) × 2.5 kg = $7.50
       You would save $7.50.

13. $\frac{1,140¢}{30¢} = 38$ days
    $1.20 × 38 = $45.60
    Mark saved $45.60.

14. a. Cost of an orange ⟶ $\frac{\$2.10}{3} = \$0.70$
       Cost of a mango ⟶ $0.70 × 4 = $2.80
       The cost of an orange is $0.70 and the cost
       of a mango is $2.80.
    b. $30.80 − $2.80 × 8 = $8.40
       Number of oranges Fiona bought = $\frac{840}{70} = 12$
       Total number of fruits bought = 8 + 12 = 20
       $\frac{\text{Number of oranges}}{\text{Total number of fruits}} = \frac{12}{12 + 8} = \frac{3}{5}$

15. a. (1.75 kg + 0.5 kg) ÷ 3 = 0.75 kg
       0.75 kilogram of flour was needed for each
       loaf of bread.
    b. 0.75 × 10 × $0.90 = $6.75
       Mrs. Belen would pay $6.75 for the flour
       needed to bake 10 loaves of bread.

Put on Your Thinking Cap!

1. Thinking skill: Analyzing parts and whole
   Strategy: Solve part of the problem
   Solution:
   12 − 9 = 3 books
   Thickness of 12 books
   = 9 × 9.5 cm = 85.5 cm
   Remaining thickness
   = 120 cm − 85.5 cm = 34.5 cm
   Thickness of each book
   = 34.5 cm ÷ 3 = 11.5 cm
   Each book is 11.5 centimeters thick.

2. Thinking skill: Analyzing parts and whole

Strategy: Solve part of the problem

Solution:

$\frac{4}{5} \div 5 = \frac{4}{25}$

Each sibling pays $\frac{4}{25}$ of the cost of the present.

$\frac{1}{5} - \frac{4}{25} = \frac{1}{25}$

$\frac{1}{25}$ of the cost of the present is $9.50.

$9.50 \times 25 = $237.50

The cost of the present is $237.50.

3. Thinking skill: Analyzing parts and whole

Strategy: Solve part of the problem

Solution:

1 carton = 2 cups

3 cups + 2 cartons = 1.8 L

3 cups + 4 cups = 1.8 L

$\qquad$ 7 cups = 1.8 L

$\qquad$ 1 cup $= \frac{1.8\ L}{7}$

$\qquad\qquad \approx 0.26$ L

The capacity of a cup is about 0.26 liter.

4. Thinking skill: Analyzing parts and whole

Strategy: Solve part of the problem

Solution:

4M + 7J $\longrightarrow$ 2.38 kg

2M + 3J $\longrightarrow$ 1.1 kg

4M + 6J $\longrightarrow$ 2.2 kg

$\qquad$ 1J $\longrightarrow$ 2.38 kg − 2.2 kg = 0.18 kg

$\qquad$ 3J $\longrightarrow$ 0.18 kg × 3 = 0.54 kg

$\qquad$ 2M $\longrightarrow$ 1.1 kg − 0.54 kg = 0.56 kg

0.56 kg ÷ 2 = 0.28 kg

The mass of a carton of milk is 0.28 kilogram.

5. Thinking skill: Analyzing parts and whole

Strategy: Use a model

Solution:

a. $12.50 ÷ 10 = $1.25

$1.25 × 3 = $3.75

Each cup of coffee cost $3.75.

b. $1.25 × 8 = $10

Leon paid $10 for 2 cups of coffee and 1 cup of tea.

6. Thinking skill: Analyzing parts and whole

Strategy: Solve part of the problem

Solution:

9 cans of mango juice = 6 cans of orange juice

$\qquad\qquad\qquad\qquad$ = 6 cans of mango juice

$\qquad\qquad\qquad\qquad\quad$ + (0.16 kg × 6)

3 cans of mango juice = 0.16 kg × 6

$\qquad\qquad\qquad\qquad$ = 0.96 kg

a. 0.96 kg ÷ 3 = 0.32 kg

The mass of each can of mango juice is 0.32 kilogram.

b. 0.32 kg + 0.16 kg = 0.48 kg

The mass of each can of orange juice is 0.48 kilogram.

7. Thinking skill: Analyzing parts and whole

Strategy: Use a model

Solution:

1 pen $\longrightarrow$ 3 notebooks

1 notebook + $3.70 $\longrightarrow$ 3 notebooks

2 notebooks $\longrightarrow$ $3.70

a. $3.70 ÷ 2 = $1.85

Each notebook cost $1.85.

b. $1.85 + $3.70 = $5.55

Each pen cost $5.55.

8. Thinking skill: Analyzing parts and whole

Strategy: Use a model

Solution:

$0.8 = \dfrac{4}{5}$

Chicken sandwich ▯▯▯▯

Cheese sandwich ▯▯▯▯▯

$4 \times 9 = 36$ units
$5 \times 7 = 35$ units
$36 + 35 = 71$ units
71 units ⟶ $46.15
1 unit ⟶ $46.15 ÷ 71 = $0.65
a. $0.65 × 4 = $2.60
   The cost of each chicken sandwich is $2.60.
b. $0.65 × 5 = $3.25
   The cost of each cheese sandwich is $3.25.

9. Thinking skill: Comparing

Strategy: Simplify the problem

Solution:
Difference in the price of an alarm clock
= $16.00 − $15.50 = $0.50 (gained)
Difference in price of a patch
= $2.30 − $2.00 = $0.30 (lost)
3 alarm clocks ⟶ gained $1.50
5 patches ⟶ lost $1.50
5 patches (loss) ⟶ 3 alarm clocks (gain)
30 patches (loss) ⟶ 18 alarm clocks (gain)
James sold 18 alarm clocks.

10. Thinking skill: Comparing

Strategy: Make a table

Solution:

Method 1:

Number of Days	Jessica	Sarah	Difference in Amount
10	0	$1.50 × 10 = $15	—
20	$2.50 × 10 = $25	$1.50 × 20 = $30	—
30	$2.50 × 20 = $50	$1.50 × 30 = $45	$5
35	$50 + $12.50 = $62.50	$45 + $7.50 = $52.50	$10
37	$62.50 + $5 = $67.50	$52.50 + $3 = $55.50	$12

a. Sarah has been saving for 37 days.
b. Jessica has saved $67.50 so far.

Method 2:

From Day 1 to Day 10, Sarah saved
$1.50 × 10 = $15
($15 + $12) ÷ $1 = 27 days
a. 10 + 27 = 37
   Sarah has been saving for 37 days.
b. $2.50 × 27 = $67.50
   Jessica has saved $67.50 so far.

11. Thinking skill: Analyzing parts and whole

Strategy: Use a model

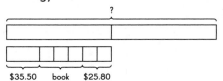

2 units ⟶ $25.80
5 units ⟶ ($25.80 ÷ 2) × 5
          = $64.50
Half of monthly allowance = $64.50 + $35.50
                          = $100
     Monthly allowance = $100 × 2
                        = $200
Albert's monthly allowance was $200.

12.

Chicken Sandwiches ▯▯▯▯▯▯▯▯▯▯▯▯▯▯▯▯ ⎫
Apple Pies ▯▯▯▯▯▯▯▯▯ ⎬ $12.50

25 units ⟶ $12.50
 1 unit ⟶ $12.50 ÷ 25
          = $0.50
1 chicken sandwich = $0.50 × 4
                   = $2
1 chicken sandwich is $2.

Chapter 10

Lesson 10.1

1. 0.5; 50%
2. 0.25; 25%
3. 0.2; 20%
4. $\dfrac{3}{10}$; 30%
5. $\dfrac{9}{20}$; 45%
6. $\dfrac{8}{25}$; 32%
7. $\dfrac{3}{4}$; 0.75
8. $\dfrac{3}{5}$; 0.6
9. $\dfrac{3}{20}$; 0.15

10. a. $100\% - 84\% = 16\%$

   16% of the questions were not completed by Jerry.

   b. $\dfrac{84}{100} = \dfrac{21}{25}$

   Jerry completed $\dfrac{21}{25}$ of the questions.

11. $1 - \dfrac{36}{100} = \dfrac{64}{100}$

   64% of the students are boys.

Lesson 10.2

1. 50   2. 25   3. 40   4. 37.5
5. 62.5   6. 55   7. 64   8. 74
9. 24   10. 46   11. 90   12. 88

13. $300 - 240 = 60$

   $\dfrac{60}{300} \times 100 = 20\%$

   20% of the participants did not complete their drawings.

14. $250 - 60 = 190$

   $190 \div 2 = 95$

   $\dfrac{95}{250} \times 100\% = 38\%$

   38% of the beads in the box are yellow.

15. Amount of money Maria spent
   $= \$6.75 + \$1.25 = \$8$

   Amount of money Maria had at first
   $= \$8 + \$12 = \$20$

   $\dfrac{8}{20} \times 100\% = 40\%$

   Maria spent 40% of her money.

16. Number of big marbles $= 45 \times 4 = 180$
   Number of small marbles $= 24 \times 5 = 120$
   Total number of marbles $= 180 + 120 = 300$

   $\dfrac{180}{300} = \dfrac{60}{100} = 60\%$

   60% of the marbles are big.

17. Indian [ ][ ][ ]
   British [ ][ ][ ][ ]

   8 units ⟶ $100\% - 52\% = 48\%$
   1 unit ⟶ $48\% \div 8 = 6\%$
   3 units ⟶ $3 \times 6\% = 18\%$
   $18\% \times 450 = 81$
   a. Glen has 81 Indian stamps.
   b. $5 \times 6\% = 30\%$
      30% of his collection are British stamps.

18. Strawberry pie [ ][ ][ ][ ][ ]
   Apple pie [ ][ ][ ] 24 pies

   1 unit ⟶ 24 pies
   9 units ⟶ $24 \times 9 = 216$ pies
   $144 + 216 = 360$
   $\dfrac{144}{360} = \dfrac{40}{100} = 40\%$

   40% of the pies are blueberry pies.

Lesson 10.3

1. $90
2. 18 h
3. 96 km
4. 4,480 people
5. 3.6 kg
6. 711 mL
7. $100\% - 30\% - 45\% = 25\%$
   $25\% \times 480 = 120$
   There are 120 roses in the shop.
8. $20\% \times 350 = 70$ girls at first
   New number of girls $= 70 + 50 = 120$
   New number of students $= 350 + 50 = 400$

   $\dfrac{120}{400} \times 100\% = 30\%$

   30% of students in the hall are girls now.

Lesson 10.4

1. Interest in 1 year ⟶ 2% of $30,000
   $= \dfrac{2}{100} \times \$30,000$
   $= \$600$
   $\$30,000 + \$600 = \$30,600$
   Leon withdrew $30,600.

2. Price of 1 flower $= \$10 \div 4 = \$2.50$
   Price of 12 flowers $= 12 \times \$2.50$
   $= \$30$
   During the sale, price of 1 flower
   $= 80\%$ of $2.50 = \$2$
   $30 \div 2 = 15$ flowers
   Mrs. Watson could buy 15 flowers with the amount of money she usually spends.

3. $432 ÷ 12 = $36

    $114 + $36 = $150

    $\frac{36}{150} \times 100\% = 24\%$

    Peter saves 24% of his allowance every month.

4.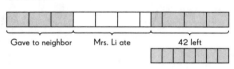

    Dress   Shoes $60 + $132

    4 units → $60 + $132 = $192

    5 units → $\frac{$192}{4} \times 5 = 240

    60% of her money → $240

    100% of her money = $\frac{$240}{60} \times 100 = 400

    Cheryl had $400 at first.

Put on Your Thinking Cap!

1. Thinking skill: Analyzing parts and whole

    Strategy: Use a model

    Solution:

    Gave to neighbor   Mrs. Li ate   42 left

    7 units → 42 crackers
    1 unit → 6 crackers
    20 units → 6 × 20 = 120 crackers
    Mrs. Li bought 120 crackers.

2. Thinking skill: Analyzing parts and whole

    Strategy: Use a model

    Solution:

    $80\% = \frac{4}{5}$

    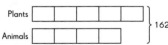

    Plants
    Animals   } 162

    9 units → 162 aquatic plants and animals

    4 units → $\frac{162}{9} \times 4 = 72$ aquatic animals

    There are 72 aquatic animals in the eco-garden.

3. Thinking skill: Analyzing parts and whole

    Strategy: Use before and after concept

    Solution:

    Before:

    Female → 60% of 150 = $\frac{60}{100} \times 150 = 90$

    a. 150 − 90 = 60

    There were 60 male goldfish.

    After:

    60

    | 52% | 48% |
    | Female | Male |

    48% → 60

    52% → $\frac{60}{48} \times 52 = 65$

    b. 90 − 65 = 25

    25 female goldfish died.

4. Thinking skill: Analyzing parts and whole

    Strategy: Use before and after concept

    Solution:

    Before:

    $40\% \times 280 = \frac{40}{100} \times 280 = 112$

    There were 112 corn muffins.
    280 − 112 = 168
    There were 168 other muffins.

    After:

    40% → 168 (other muffins)

    60% → $\frac{168}{40} \times 60 = 252$ (corn muffins)

    252 − 112 = 140

    Mr. Parker must bake 140 more corn muffins.

Test Prep for Chapters 8 to 10

1. D   2. C
3. C   4. B
5. D   6. C
7. C   8. D
9. C   10. A

11. $7\frac{1}{4}$ 12. 6.85

13. 2.65   14. 1.56

15. 22.50   16. 5

17. 72.67 ≈ 73

18. Mother's age = 9 × 4 = 36 years
   Ivy's age 9 years from now
   = 9 + 9 = 18 years
   Mother's age 9 years from now
   36 + 9 = 45 years
   Ivy's age as a percent of her mother's age
   9 years from now
   $= \dfrac{18}{45} \times 100\% = 40\%$

19. Total number of students who scored an A
   = 20% × 300 = 60
   Remaining students = 300 − 60 = 240
   Total number of students who scored a B
   = 45% × 240 = 108

20. Total percent of boys
   = 100% − 40% − 5% = 55%
   Difference between percent of boys and girls
   $= 55\% - 40\% = 15\% = \dfrac{3}{20}$

   3 units ➞ 270
   1 unit ➞ 90
   90 adults participated in the survey.

21.
Tennis racket					

   | Badminton racket | | | | | $7.60 |

   1 unit ➞ $7.60
   4 units ➞ $7.60 × 4 = $30.40
   The cost of the badminton racket is $30.40.

22. 13 units ➞ 100% − 48% = 52%
   1 unit ➞ 4%
   8 units ➞ 32% (apples)
   5 units ➞ 20% (pears)
   48% − 32% = 16%
   16% ➞ 128
   4% ➞ 32
   20% ➞ 32 × 5 = 160
   There are 160 pears in the basket.

23. **Before:**
   apple pies ➞ 55% × 160 = 88
   cherry pies ➞ 160 − 88 = 72
   After:
   60% ➞ 72
   100% ➞ 120
   a. 120 pies were left.
      120 − 72 = 48
      48 apple pies were left.
   b. 88 − 48 = 40
      40 apple pies were sold.

Chapter 11

Lesson 11.1

1. 700 + 600 = 1,300

2. 700 − 300 = 400

3. $\dfrac{300}{900} = \dfrac{1}{3}$

4. Total = 600 + 400 = 1,000
   $\dfrac{600}{1,000} \times 100\% = 60\%$

5. A : B : D = 400 : 600 : 800 = 2 : 3 : 4

6.
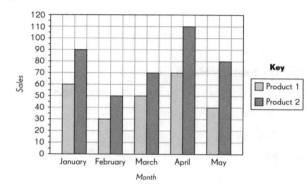

7. (60 + 30 + 50 + 70 + 40) ÷ 5 = 50

8. January : May = 60 : 40 = 3 : 2

9. February;
   90 − 50 = 40

10. Total sales = 90 + 50 + 70 + 110 + 80
    = 400
    $\dfrac{80}{400} \times 100\% = 20\%$

Lesson 11.2

1. (3, 7)   2. (0, 4)   3. (4, 0)

4. (1, 8)   5. (5, 2)   6. (6, 1)

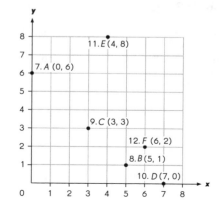

13. 9 ft   14. 16.5 ft

15. 4 yd   16. 7 yd

17. Y = 6.5; F = 19.5

18. Width (W) inch: 4; 6
    Length (L) inch: 10; 16

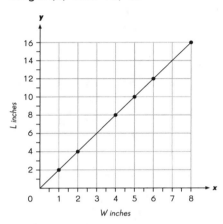

19. 6   20. 11

21. 3   22. 7

Lesson 11.3

1.

Sizes \ Pies	fish	beef	chicken	mushroom
small	small fish	small beef	small chicken	small mushroom
medium	medium fish	medium beef	medium chicken	medium mushroom
large	large fish	large beef	large chicken	large mushroom

$3 \times 4 = 12$

She can bake 12 different pies.

2.

Manual 1600 c.c. blue	Automatic 1600 c.c. blue
Manual 1600 c.c. white	Automatic 1600 c.c. white
Manual 1600 c.c. grey	Automatic 1600 c.c. grey
Manual 2000 c.c. blue	Automatic 2000 c.c. blue
Manual 2000 c.c. white	Automatic 2000 c.c. white
Manual 2000 c.c. grey	Automatic 2000 c.c. grey

$2 \times 2 \times 3 = 12$

Mr. Samuel needs to consider 12 combinations.

3. Let A, B, C, D, E, and F represent 6 people
(Ms. Beckham and her 5 friends).
A shakes hands with B, C, D, E, F = 5 handshakes
B shakes hands with C, D, E, F = 4 handshakes
C shakes hands with D, E, F = 3 handshakes
D shakes hands with E, F = 2 handshakes
E shakes hands with F = 1 handshake
Total number = 1 + 2 + 3 + 4 + 5 = 15
There are 15 handshakes.

4. Make a list in order:
V S F   V S A   V S I
V F F   V F A   V F I
V L F   V L A   V L I
C S F   C S A   C S I
C F F   C F A   C F I
C L F   C L A   C L I
M S F   M S A   M S I
M F F   M F A   M F I
M L F   M L A   M L I
9 + 9 + 9 = 27
The restaurant has 27 different three-course meals.

Lesson 11.4

1. $\frac{1}{4}$ 2. 1   3. $\frac{1}{4}$ 4. $\frac{1}{3}$

5. Answers vary.   6. Answers vary.

7. Answers vary.   8. Answers vary.

9. Answers vary.

10.

			1st cube			
+	1	2	3	4	5	6
1	2	3	4	5	6	7
2	3	4	5	6	7	8
3	4	5	6	7	8	9
4	5	6	7	8	9	10
5	6	7	8	9	10	11
6	7	8	9	10	11	12

(2nd cube labels the rows)

11. 7; Answer varies.

12. 2 or 12; Answer varies.

13. $\frac{5}{36}$ 14. $\frac{9}{40}$

© 2009 Marshall Cavendish International (Singapore) Private Limited. Copying is permitted; see page ii.

15. $\frac{1}{5}$ 16. $\frac{3}{10}$

17. $\frac{11}{40}$ 18. $\frac{1}{4}$

Put on Your Thinking Cap!

1. Thinking skill: Induction

   Solution: Answers vary.

2. Thinking skill: Induction

   Strategy: Make suppositions

   Solution: Answers vary.

Chapter 12

Lesson 12.1

1. 55°   2. 53°   3. 56°   4. 90°

Lesson 12.2

1. 136°   2. 131°   3. 84°

4. $m\angle d = 62°$; $m\angle e = 124°$

Lesson 12.3

1. 97°   2. 35°   3. 142°   4. 24°

5. Angles at a Point:

   $\angle e$, $\angle f$, $\angle m$, and $\angle n$; $\angle i$, $\angle g$, $\angle h$, and $\angle p$; $\angle j$, $\angle k$, $\angle r$, and $\angle q$

   Vertical Angles:

   $\angle a$ and $\angle c$; $\angle e$ and $\angle n$; $\angle f$ and $\angle m$; $\angle i$ and $\angle p$; $\angle g$ and $\angle h$; $\angle j$ and $\angle q$; $\angle k$ and $\angle r$

   Angles on a Line:

   $\angle a$ and $\angle d$; $\angle a$ and $\angle b$; $\angle c$ and $\angle d$; $\angle f$ and $\angle n$; $\angle e$ and $\angle m$; $\angle e$ and $\angle f$; $\angle m$ and $\angle n$; $\angle i$ and $\angle h$; $\angle g$ and $\angle p$; $\angle i$ and $\angle g$; $\angle h$ and $\angle p$; $\angle j$ and $\angle r$; $\angle k$ and $\angle q$; $\angle j$ and $\angle k$; $\angle r$ and $\angle q$

6. 138°   7. 147°

Put on Your Thinking Cap!

1. Thinking skill: Spatial visualization

   Solution:

   $m\angle x = 90° - 49° = 41°$

2. Thinking skill: Spatial visualization

   Solution:

   $m\angle x + m\angle y + m\angle z = 180°$

   $m\angle x = 180° - 142° = 38°$

   $m\angle y = 180° - 94° = 86°$

   $m\angle z = 180° - 124° = 56°$

3. Thinking skill: Spatial visualization

   Solution:

   $m\angle x + m\angle y = (51° \div 3) \times 7 = 119°$

   $m\angle z = 360° - 119° = 241°$

4. Thinking skill: Spatial visualization

   Solution:

   $m\angle x + m\angle y \longrightarrow 7$ units $= 180° - 54° = 126°$

   $m\angle y = (126° \div 7) \times 2 = 36°$

   $m\angle z = 180° - 36° - 38° = 106°$

5. Thinking skill: Spatial visualization

   Solution:

   $m\angle p + m\angle q + m\angle r \longrightarrow 12$ units $= 180°$

   $m\angle p = (180° \div 12) \times 7 = 105°$

   $m\angle r = (180° \div 12) \times 4 = 60°$

6. Thinking skill: Spatial visualization

   Solution:

   $m\angle a + m\angle b + m\angle c \longrightarrow 12$ units

   $\qquad\qquad = 360° - 132°$

   $\qquad\qquad = 228°$

   $m\angle a = (228° \div 12) \times 3 = 57°$

   $m\angle b = (228° \div 12) \times 4 = 76°$

   $m\angle c = (228° \div 12) \times 5 = 95°$

7. Thinking skill: Spatial visualization

   Solution:

   $\angle a$ ▢▢

   $\angle d$ ▢▢▢

   $\angle b$ ▢▢▢▢

   $\angle c$ ▢▢▢▢▢▢▢▢▢

   18 units $\longrightarrow$ 360°

   1 unit $\longrightarrow$ 360° $\div$ 18 = 20°

   $m\angle a = 20° \times 2 = 40°$

   $m\angle b = 20° \times 4 = 80°$

   $m\angle c = 20° \times 9 = 180°$

   $m\angle d = 20° \times 3 = 60°$

8. Thinking skill: Spatial visualization

   Solution:

   $m\angle AOE = 180° - 108° = 72°$

   $m\angle AOC = 130° - 72° = 58°$

   $m\angle BOC = 90° - 58° = 32°$

   $m\angle BOD = m\angle AOC = 58°$

   $m\angle DOF = 90° - 58° = 32°$

   $m\angle BOC$ and $m\angle DOF$ are equal.

Chapter 13

Lesson 13.1

1. Scalene triangles: *LMN*; *XYZ*; *STU*
   Equilateral triangles: *ABC*; *PQR*
   Isosceles triangles: *DEF*; *GHK*; *KFC*

2. Right triangles: *DEF*; *LMN*; *XYZ*
   Equilateral triangles: *GHK*; *STU*
   Isosceles triangles: *ABC*; *PQR*; *VWX*

Lesson 13.2

1. 96° 2. 26° 3. 133° 4. 59°
5. 62° 6. 251° 7. 25° 8. 67°

Lesson 13.3

1. 32° 2. 53° 3. 101° 4. 29°
5. 33° 6. 30° 7. 120° 8. 106°

Lesson 13.4

1. 2; 2; 3   2. 4
3. 5   4. 5
5. Yes   6. Yes
7. Yes   8. 6; 3; 5
9. 9   10. 8
11. 11   12. *AC*
13. *BC*   14. *AB*
15. Answers vary. Accept any possible answer:
    3 in., 4 in., or 5 in.
16. Answers vary. Accept any possible answer:
    5 cm, 6 cm, 7 cm, or 8 cm
17. Answers vary. Accept any possible answer:
    2 cm, 3 cm, 4 cm 5 cm, 6 cm, 7 cm, 8 cm,
    or 9 cm
18. 4 inches

Lesson 13.5

1. 16°   2. 118°; 62°
3. 131°   4. 116°
5. 154°   6. 44°
7. 76°   8. 46°

Put on Your Thinking Cap!

1. Thinking skill: Spatial visualization
   Solution:
   $m\angle UPT = 180° - 118° = 62°$
   $m\angle PUT = (180° - 62°) \div 2 = 59°$
   $m\angle TUV = m\angle TSV = 118° - 59° = 59°$
   $m\angle RSV = 118° - 59° = 59°$

2. Thinking skill: Spatial visualization
   Solution:
   $m\angle QPS = m\angle PST = 106°$
   $m\angle SPT = (180° - 106°) \div 2 = 37°$
   $m\angle a = 180° - 106° - 37° = 37°$

3. Thinking skill: Spatial visualization
   Solution:
   $m\angle FDE = 180° - 54° = 126°$
   $m\angle ADE = 126° \div 2 = 63°$
   $m\angle CDE = 90° - 63° = 27°$

4. Thinking skill: Spatial visualization
   Solution:
   $m\angle ABC = (180° - 32°) \div 2 = 74°$
   $m\angle x = 180° - 74° = 106°$
   $m\angle x = m\angle AFE = 106°$
   $m\angle y = (180° - 106°) \div 2 = 37°$

5. Thinking skill: Spatial visualization
   Solution:
   $m\angle PRQ = 180° - 27° \times 2 = 126°$
   $m\angle PRS = 180° - 126° = 54°$
   $m\angle x = 180° - 54° \times 2 = 72°$
   $3 \times m\angle TPS = 180° - 72° - 27° - 27° = 54°$
   $m\angle TPS = 18°$
   $m\angle STP = 2 \times 18° = 36°$
   $m\angle y = 180° - 36° = 144°$

6. Thinking skill: Spatial visualization
   Solution:
   $m\angle CEF = (180° - 118°) \div 2 = 31°$
   $m\angle x = 180° - 60° - 60° - 31° = 29°$
   $m\angle FEG = 180° - 31° - 54° = 95°$
   $m\angle EFG = 180° - 118° = 62°$
   $m\angle y = 180° - 95° - 62° = 23°$

7. Thinking skill: Spatial visualization
   Solution:
   $m\angle EAF = m\angle AEF = 90° - 34° = 56°$
   $m\angle AFE = m\angle BFG = 180° - 56° \times 2 = 68°$
   $m\angle FBG = m\angle FGB = (180° - 68°) \div 2 = 56°$
   $m\angle EBA = 90° - 58° = 32°$
   $m\angle y = 56° + 32° = 88°$
   $m\angle x = 180° - 56° - 88° = 36°$

8. Thinking skill: Spatial visualization

Solution:
$m\angle ABC = m\angle CDE = 56°$
$m\angle x = 180° - 56° - 90° = 34°$
$m\angle CFD = 180° - 103° = 77°$
$m\angle DCF = 180° - 77° - 56° = 47°$
$m\angle y = 90° - 47° = 43°$

Chapter 14

Lesson 14.1

	Solid	Number of Faces (F)	Number of Vertices (V)	Number of Edges (E)
1.	cube	6	8	12
2.	rectangular prism	6	8	12
3.	triangular prism	5	6	9
4.	square pyramid	5	5	8
5.	triangular pyramid	4	4	6

6. For any prism and pyramid, subtracting the number of edges from the sum of the number of faces and the number of vertices, equals 2.

7.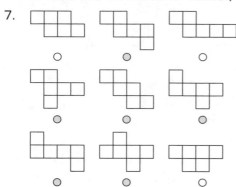

8.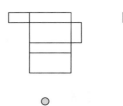

9.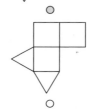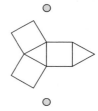

10.

11.

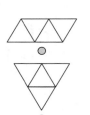 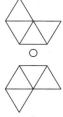

Lesson 14.2

1. 2; 1

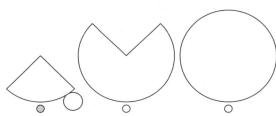

2. 1

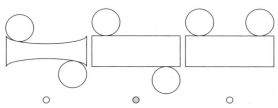

3.

(triangular pyramid)   (cone)   (sphere)

(cylinder)   (triangular prism)   (cube)

4. F
5. T
6. F
7. F
8. T
9. T

Put on Your Thinking Cap!

Thinking skill: Identifying patterns and relationship

Strategy: Look for a pattern

Solution:

	Solid	Number of Faces (F)	Number of Edges (E)	Number of Vertice (V)	F+V−E
1.	cube	6	12	8	2
2.	cone	1	0	1	2
3.	triangular prism	5	9	6	2
4.	square pyramid	5	8	5	2
5.	triangular pyramid	4	6	4	2
6.	cylinder	2	0	0	2

7. Thinking skill: Identifying patterns and relationships

Strategy: Look for a pattern

Solution:

Shape	Number of Sticks Used	Total Surface Area
4	36	18
5	44	22

8. Thinking skill: Identifying patterns and relationships

Strategy: Look for a pattern

Solution:

$8 \times 10 + 4 = 84$

84 sticks are needed to form Shape 10.

Chapter 15

Lesson 15.1

1. 8   2. 10
3. 12   4. 13
5. 10

Lesson 15.2

1.

2.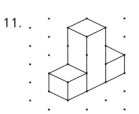

11. 12.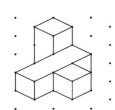

13.

14.

3. 4.

5. 6.

7.

15.

8.

9.

16.

10.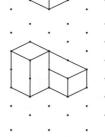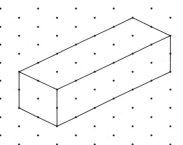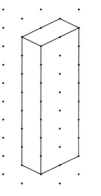

Lesson 15.3

1. $4 \text{ cm} \times 4 \text{ cm} = 16 \text{ cm}^2$
    $16 \text{ cm}^2 \times 6 = 96 \text{ cm}^2$
    The surface area of the cube is 96 square centimeters.

2. $5 \text{ cm} \times 3 \text{ cm} = 15 \text{ cm}^2$
    $3 \text{ cm} \times 2 \text{ cm} = 6 \text{ cm}^2$
    $5 \text{ cm} \times 2 \text{ cm} = 10 \text{ cm}^2$
    $(15 \text{ cm}^2 + 6 \text{ cm}^2 + 10 \text{ cm}^2) \times 2 = 62 \text{ cm}^2$
    The surface area of the rectangular prism is 62 square centimeters.

3. $5 \text{ cm} \times 5 \text{ cm} = 25 \text{ cm}^2$
    $25 \text{ cm}^2 \times 6 = 150 \text{ cm}^2$

4. $8 \text{ in.} \times 8 \text{ in.} = 64 \text{ in.}^2$
    $64 \text{ in.}^2 \times 6 = 384 \text{ in.}^2$

5. $20 \text{ cm} \times 6 \text{ cm} = 120 \text{ cm}^2$
    $10 \text{ cm} \times 6 \text{ cm} = 60 \text{ cm}^2$
    $20 \text{ cm} \times 10 \text{ cm} = 200 \text{ cm}^2$
    $(120 + 60 + 200) \text{ cm}^2 \times 2 = 760 \text{ cm}^2$

6. $10 \text{ cm} \times 10 \text{ cm} = 100 \text{ cm}^2$
    $18 \text{ cm} \times 10 \text{ cm} = 180 \text{ cm}^2$
    $100 \text{ cm}^2 \times 2 + 180 \text{ cm}^2 \times 4 = 920 \text{ cm}^2$

7. $7 \text{ in.} \times 7 \text{ in.} = 49 \text{ in.}^2$
    $49 \text{ in.}^2 \times 6 = 294 \text{ in.}^2$

8. $10 \text{ cm} \times 10 \text{ cm} = 100 \text{ cm}^2$
    $100 \text{ cm}^2 \times 6 = 600 \text{ cm}^2$

9. $10 \text{ in.} \times 9 \text{ in.} = 90 \text{ in.}^2$
    $10 \text{ in.} \times 6 \text{ in.} = 60 \text{ in.}^2$
    $9 \text{ in.} \times 6 \text{ in.} = 54 \text{ in.}^2$
    $(90 + 60 + 54) \text{ in.}^2 \times 2 = 408 \text{ in.}^2$

10. $20 \text{ cm} \times 15 \text{ cm} = 300 \text{ cm}^2$
    $20 \text{ cm} \times 10 \text{ cm} = 200 \text{ cm}^2$
    $15 \text{ cm} \times 10 \text{ cm} = 150 \text{ cm}^2$
    $(300 + 200 + 150) \text{ cm}^2 \times 2 = 1,300 \text{ cm}^2$

11. $8 \text{ in.} \times 6 \text{ in.} = 48 \text{ in.}^2$
    $8 \text{ in.} \times 12 \text{ in.} = 96 \text{ in.}^2$
    $12 \text{ in.} \times 6 \text{ in.} = 72 \text{ in.}^2$
    $(48 + 96 + 72) \text{ in.}^2 \times 2 = 432 \text{ in.}^2$

12. $12 \text{ cm} \times 12 \text{ cm} = 144 \text{ cm}^2$
    $12 \text{ cm} \times 20 \text{ cm} = 240 \text{ cm}^2$
    $144 \text{ cm}^2 \times 2 + 240 \text{ cm}^2 \times 4 = 1,248 \text{ cm}^2$

13. $216 \text{ cm}^2 \div 6 = 36 \text{ cm}^2$
    $\underline{6} \times \underline{6} = 36$
    The length of the cube is 6 centimeters.

14. $6 \text{ cm} \times 6 \text{ cm} = 36 \text{ cm}^2$
    $30 \text{ cm} \times 6 \text{ cm} = 180 \text{ cm}^2$
    $36 \text{ cm}^2 \times 2 + 180 \text{ cm}^2 \times 4 = 792 \text{ cm}^2$
    The surface area of the wood is 792 square centimeters.

15. $20 \text{ in.} \times 18 \text{ in.} = 360 \text{ in.}^2$
    $20 \text{ in.} \times 16 \text{ in.} = 320 \text{ in.}^2$
    $18 \text{ in.} \times 16 \text{ in.} = 288 \text{ in.}^2$
    $360 \text{ in.}^2 + (320 \text{ in.}^2 \times 2) + (288 \text{ in.}^2 \times 2) = 1,576 \text{ in.}^2$
    The total surface area of the tank in contact with the water is 1,576 square inches.

Lesson 15.4

1. 12
2. 9
3. 12
4. 11
5. B
6. A; C
7. 12
8. 12
9. 9
10. 17
11. G
12. H
13. E and F
14. 5; 2; 3; 30
15. 4; 3; 4; 48
16. 8; 5; 4; 160
17. 8; 6; 4; 192

Lesson 15.5

1. 8; 5; 7
    Volume = $8 \times 5 \times 7 = 280$

2. 14; 7; 10
    Volume = $14 \times 7 \times 10 = 980$

3. 32; 28; 20
    Volume = $32 \times 28 \times 20 = 17,920$

4. $25.8 \times 12 \times 18 = 5,572.8$

5. $15 \times 15 \times 28.6 = 6,435$

6. 8
7. 12
8. 18
9. 8
10. 390
11. 1,125
12. 2,600
13. 4,080
14. 5,050
15. 2,006
16. 0; 890
17. 1; 850
18. 3; 65
19. 0.53
20. 0.755
21. 1.65
22. 2.075
23. 6,552 mL
24. 7,200 mL
25. 3.24 L
26. 8.4 L

27. Volume of fish tank $= 38$ cm $\times 23$ cm $\times 18$ cm
$$= 15{,}732 \text{ cm}^3$$
$\frac{2}{3} \times 15{,}732 \text{ cm}^3 = 10{,}488 \text{ cm}^3 = 10 \text{ L } 488 \text{ mL}$
When the tank is $\frac{2}{3}$ full, there is

10 liters 488 milliliters of water in it.

28. Fraction of water left $= \frac{3}{4} \times \frac{4}{5} = \frac{3}{5}$

Volume of tank $= 30$ cm $\times 22$ cm $\times 25$ cm
$$= 16{,}500 \text{ cm}^3$$
$\frac{3}{5} \times 16{,}500 \text{ cm}^3 = 9{,}900 \text{ cm}^3 = 9.9 \text{ L}$

The volume of water left in the tank is 9.9 liters.

29. Height of water needed $= 24$ cm $- 7$ cm
$$= 17 \text{ cm}$$

Volume of water needed $= 42$ cm $\times 20$ cm
$$\times 17 \text{ cm}$$
$$= 14{,}280 \text{ cm}^3$$
$$= 14.28 \text{ L}$$
The volume of water needed is 14.28 liters.

Put on Your Thinking Cap!

1. Thinking skill: Identifying patterns and relationships
   Strategy: Look for a pattern
   Solution:
   $7 \times 7 = 49$
   Jessica will need 49 cubes.

2. Thinking skill: Identifying patterns and relationships
   Strategy: Look for a pattern
   Solution:
   a.

T-Shaped Pattern	1	2	3	4
Number of Unit Cubes	5	$5 + 3$ $= 8$	$8 + 3$ $= 11$	$11 + 3$ $= 14$

   b. Pattern 5: $14 + 3 = 17$
      Pattern 6: $17 + 3 = 20$
   c. Pattern 10: $3 \times 10 + 2 = 32$ cubes

3. Thinking skill: Spatial visualization
   Strategy: Simplify the problem
   Solution:
   Volume of each cube $= 960 \text{ cm}^3 \div 15$
   $$= 64 \text{ cm}^3$$
   4 cm $\times 4$ cm $\times 4$ cm $= 64 \text{ cm}^3$
   Length of each cube is 4 centimeters.
   The solid has 42 exposed faces.
   Surface area of solid $= 42 \times (4 \times 4) \text{ cm}^2$
   $$= 672 \text{ cm}^2$$
   The surface area that is painted blue is
   672 square centimeters.

4. Thinking skill: Spatial visualization
   Strategy: Simplify the problem
   Solution:
   $6 \times 3 = 18$ cubes (1 layer)
   $126 \div 18 = 7$ layers
   7×3 cm $= 21$ cm
   The height of the box is 21 centimeters.

5. Thinking skill: Spatial visualization
   Strategy: Simplify the problem
   Solution:
   a. $(3 \times 3 \times 3) \text{ cm}^3 \times 12 = 324 \text{ cm}^3$
      The volume of the solid is 324 cubic centimeters.
   b. The solid has 38 exposed faces.
      $38 \times (3 \times 3) \text{ cm}^2 = 342 \text{ cm}^2$
      The total surface area of the solid is 342 square centimeters.
   c. i. 2 cubes
      ii. 6 cubes
      iii. 4 cubes

6. Thinking skill: Analyzing parts and whole
   Strategy: Solve part of the problem
   Solution:
   3 units $\longrightarrow 12$ cm $\times 10$ cm $\times 6$ cm $= 720 \text{ cm}^3$
   7 units $\longrightarrow \frac{720}{3} \text{ cm}^3 \times 7 = 1{,}680 \text{ cm}^3$.
   a. The volume of block B is 1,680 cubic centimeters.
   $$\frac{1{,}680 \text{ cm}^3}{10 \text{ cm} \times 12 \text{ cm}} = 14 \text{ cm}$$
   b. The width of block B is 14 centimeters.

7. Thinking skill: Deduction

Strategy: Use a model

Solution:

12 units − 4 units = 8 units

8 units ➝ 1,024 mL

4 units ➝ 512 mL

Volume of the cubic container

= 8 cm × 8 cm × 8 cm = 512 cm^3

The length of the cubic container is 8 centimeters.

8. Thinking skill: Analyzing parts and whole

Strategy: Solve part of the problem

Solution:

Length ➝ 36 ÷ 4 = 9

Width ➝ 8 ÷ 2 = 4

Height ➝ 21 ÷ 3 = 7

Total number of blocks needed = 9 × 4 × 7

                               = 252

$\frac{4}{9} \times 252 = 112$

John will need 112 blocks to complete the wall.

9. Thinking skill: Comparing, Spatial visualization

Strategy: Simplify the problem

Solution:

Length ➝ 25 ÷ 2 is about 12

Width ➝ 15 ÷ 2 is about 7

Height ➝ 20 ÷ 2 = 10

Number of cubes = 12 × 7 × 10 = 840

840 cubes can be packed into the prism.

10. Thinking skill: Comparing, Spatial visualization

Strategy: Simplify the problem

Solution:

Length ➝ 54 ÷ 6 = 9

Width ➝ 44 ÷ 8 is about 5

Height ➝ 22 ÷ 10 is about 2

9 × 5 × 2 = 90

The maximum number of watch boxes that can be packed into the container is 90.

11. Thinking skill: Analyzing parts and whole, Deduction

Strategy: Simplify the problem

Solution:

a. Dimensions: 5 cm by 5 cm by 12 cm

b. Dimensions: 3 cm by 3 cm by 20 cm
   Accept possible drawings.

c. Volume of one solid
   = 5 cm × 5 cm × 12 cm = 300 cm^3
   Volume of the other solid
   = 20 cm × 3 cm × 3 cm = 180 cm^3

End-of-Year Test

Multiple choice

1. C	2. C	3. C	4. C
5. B	6. D	7. B	8. A
9. B	10. C	11. B	12. D
13. B	14. A	15. C	16. A
17. C	18. D	19. B	20. B

Short Answer

21. Factors of 6 are: 1, 2, 3, and 6.

    $\frac{4}{8} = \frac{1}{2}$

22. 19.4

23. $6\frac{7}{30}$

24. $2d + 6$

25. $19y - 6$

26. 5 × 10 = 50

27. $\frac{7}{8}$ kg × $\frac{3}{5}$ = $\frac{21}{40}$ kg

    $\frac{21}{40}$ kilogram of beef is left.

28. $\frac{2}{7} \times \frac{3}{4} = \frac{3}{14}$

    $\frac{3}{14} \times 84 = 18$

    Karen gets 18 beads.

29. $\frac{38}{0.2} = 190$

30. Photo B measures 16 cm by 12 cm.

    16 cm × 12 cm = 192 cm²

    The area of Photo B is 192 square centimeters.

31. Area of shaded region

    $= \frac{1}{2} \times 26 \times (20 - 10) = 130$ cm²

32. Surface area of the rectangular prism

    = (12 + 8) × 2 × 6 + 12 × 8 × 2

    = 432 cm²

33. Volume of each cube = $\frac{1{,}620}{60}$ = 27 cm³

    Length of each cube = L × L × L = 27 cm³

    L = 3 cm

34. Volume of water

    = 24 cm × 20 cm × 15 cm = $7\frac{1}{5}$ L

35. 3 L

36. Total number of computers sold

    = 35 + 30 + 40 + 25 + 45 = 175

37. Shop 4

    40 − 25 = 15 (increase)

38. 180° − 35° × 2 = 110°

    m∠ACD = 110° − 60° = 50°

39. (180° − 86°) ÷ 2 = 47°

    m∠RQT = 180° − 86° − 47° − 28° = 19°

40. 58° − 23° = 35°

    (180° − 42°) ÷ 2 = 69°

    180° − 69° = 111°

    m∠AEF = 180° − 111° − 35° = 34°

41. $95 − $75 = $20

    40% ➞ $20

    100% ➞ $50 (his savings)

    $95 + $50 = $145

    Lincoln has $145 every month.

42.

Area (cm²)	Common Factors
40, 25	1, 5
40, 32	1, 2, 4, 8
25, 30	1, 5

By deduction,

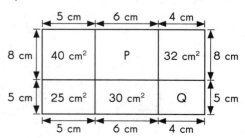

Length of P = 8 cm

Width of P = 6 cm

Length of Q = 5 cm

Width of Q = 4 cm.

Area of P ➞ 8 × 6 = 48 cm²

Area of Q ➞ 5 × 4 = 20 cm²

48 cm² + 20 cm² = 68 cm²

a. The total area of P and Q is 68 square centimeters.

   (13 cm + 15 cm) × 2 = 56 cm

b. The perimeter of the figure is 56 centimeters.

43.

	A	B	C
Before:	3	5	2
After:	$1\frac{1}{2}$	$5\frac{1}{2}$	3

1 unit ➞ 18

18 × 3 = 54

a. Alex had 54 marbles before the game.

   18 × 5.5 = 99

b. Benny had 99 marbles at the end of the game.

44.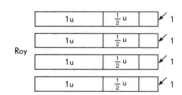

    $\frac{1}{2}$ unit ➞ 16 − 1 = 15

    1 unit ➞ 15 × 2 = 30

    30 × 6 + 4 = 184

    Roy had 184 stamps in the end.

45.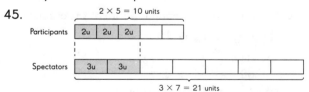

a. The number of participants is $\frac{10}{21}$ of the number of spectators.

   11 units ➞ 253

   1 unit ➞ 253 ÷ 11 = 23

   23 × 21 = 483

b. 483 spectators were at the meet.